COACHI

The ASTD Trainer's Sourcebook

Books in The ASTD Trainer's Sourcebook Series

COACHING:

The ASTD Trainer's Sourcebook

Dennis C. Kinlaw

McGraw-Hill

New York San Francisco Washington D.C. Auckland Bogotá
Caracas Lisbon London Madrid Mexico City Milan
Montreal New Delhi San Juan Singapore
Sydney Tokyo Toronto

Library of Congress Catalog Card Number: 95-076448

McGraw-Hill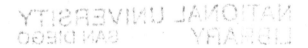

A Division of The McGraw-Hill Companies

1 2 3 4 5 6 7 8 9   MAL/MAL   9 0 0 9 8 7 6 5

ISBN: 0-07-053443-8

Sourcebook Team:

Co-Publishers:	Philip Ruppel, Training McGraw-Hill
	Nancy Olson, American Society for Training and Development
Acquisitions Editor:	Richard Narramore, Training McGraw-Hill
Editing Supervisor:	Paul R. Sobel, McGraw-Hill Professional Book Group
Production Supervisor:	Pamela A. Pelton, McGraw-Hill Professional Book Group
Series Advisor:	Richard L. Roe
Editing/Imagesetting:	Claire Condra Arias, Stacy Marquardt
	Ellipsys International Publications, Inc.

Contents

Preface

I'd like to tell you how this series came about. As a long-time editor and resource person in the field of human resources development, I was frequently asked by trainers, facilitators, consultants, and instructors to provide them with training designs on a variety of topics. These customers wanted one-hour, half-day, and full-day programs on such topics as team-building, coaching, diversity, supervision, and sales. Along with the training designs, they required facilitator notes, participant handouts, flipchart ideas, games, activities, structured experiences, overhead transparencies, and instruments. But, that wasn't all. They wanted to be able to reproduce, customize, and adapt these materials to their particular needs—at no cost!

Later, as an independent editor, I shared these needs with Nancy Olson, the publisher at the American Society for Training and Development. Nancy mentioned that ASTD received many similar calls from facilitators who were looking for a basic library of reproducible training materials. Many of the classic training volumes, such as Jones and Pfeiffer's *Handbook of Structured Experiences* and Newstrom and Scannell's *Games Trainers Play* provided a variety of useful activities. However, they lacked training designs, handouts, overheads, and instruments—and, most importantly, they tended to be organized by method rather than by topic. You can guess the rest of the story: Welcome to *The ASTD Trainer's Sourcebook*.

This sourcebook is part of an open-ended series that covers the training topics most often found in many organizations. Instead of locking you into a prescribed "workbook mentality," this sourcebook will free you from having to buy more workbooks each time you present training. This volume contains everything you need—background information on the topic, facilitator notes, training designs, participant handouts, activities, instruments, flipcharts, overheads, and resources—and it's all reproducible! We welcome you to adapt it to your particular needs. Please photocopy. . . edit . . . add your name . . . add your client's name. Please don't tell us . . . it isn't necessary! Enjoy.

Richard L. Roe
ASTD Sourcebook Series Advisor

COACHING:

The ASTD Trainer's Sourcebook

Chapter One:

Introduction

Welcome to *COACHING: The ASTD Trainer's Sourcebook*—your one-stop reference for coaching training materials.

> ### COACHING:
> ### THE ASTD TRAINER'S SOURCEBOOK:
>
> This chapter describes the contents and structure of the book. It also shows you how to navigate through the material, and select the building blocks needed to create your own coaching training program. This chapter contains the following topics:
>
> - Purposes of this Sourcebook.
> - Sourcebook Organization.
> - Workshop Building Blocks.
> - Subject/Reference Matrix.
> - Navigating the Training Plans.
> - Understanding the Icons.
> - Formula for Superior Coaching.

Over the past ten years, the roles and functions of supervisors and managers have changed so dramatically that organizations have found it necessary to search for new names to describe accurately the job of these leaders. Names like team leader, regional coach, coaching supervisor, and lead associate have become more and more common. Whether these names, and other such innovations, will finally replace the more traditional titles of manager and supervisor, it is impossible to tell, but the traditional work of managers and supervisors is rapidly disappearing. Two new roles, and their accompanying sets of functions, are clearly becoming more and more dominant. These are team leader and coach.

Human resource development (HRD) professionals are being required more and more to train organizational leaders to be coaches. The purpose of this sourcebook is to make it as easy as possible for trainers and other HRD professionals to help organizational leaders become committed to the role of coach and begin to acquire the understanding and skills to be successful coaches.

Purposes of This Sourcebook

There are a number of existing resources that can be of considerable use to trainers in designing and conducting training. None of these, however, achieve the purposes of this sourcebook.

The general intent of this sourcebook is to provide trainers a single resource they can use to enter easily and quickly into the business of designing and delivering successful coaching training for leaders at all levels, in any organization. We do not mean to suggest that what you will find in the following pages is a cookbook about coaching. You will not find simple-minded recipes you can follow by rote to cook up a successful coaching program. What you will find is material to help you understand fully what coaching is, why coaching skills are critical to the successful performance of organizational leaders, and the materials necessary for translating your understanding into successful coaching training programs.

The specific purposes of this sourcebook are to give you:

- A clear and concrete understanding of the meaning of coaching.

- Guidance for planning and preparing to deliver coaching skills programs.

- Designs for coaching training programs of one-hour, half-day, one-day, two-days, and three-days.

- All the learning activities and visual aids that you need to deliver your coaching training programs.

- Notes for conducting each of the coaching training programs.

- Assessment tools to enrich your coaching training programs.

- A list of references of additional resources.

Our expectation is that, if you use the information we give you about coaching, and if you follow the suggestions we make for planning and delivering coaching training programs, you will be successful in delivering these programs. We also expect that once you have begun to use the materials included in this sourcebook and deliver the programs, you will begin to create your own materials and discover many ways to make your coaching skills training programs your very own.

Sourcebook Organization

This sourcebook has eleven chapters and an appendix containing annotated references. A brief description of each chapter follows:

1. Introduction

The first chapter introduces you to the content of this sourcebook and provides a Subject/Chapter Matrix for finding and familiarizing yourself with the materials.

2. Background

Chapter Two provides essential background material needed to understand coaching and the conceptual framework for the training plans. It also helps you understand the meaning of coaching and introduces you to the *Superior Coaching Model*. The model provides a clear and graphic description of superior coaching skills training programs described in Chapters 4 through 8. The chapter also contains a glossary of key terms.

3. Workshop Preparation

Chapter Three gives general tips on workshop preparation, including how to design, administer, facilitate, conduct, and follow up on the training program.

4. One-Hour Coaching Programs

Coaching skills training must be an ongoing skills training program if we want coaching behavior to become an expected and accepted aspect of people's performance. It is recognized, however, that trainers may need to deliver quite brief programs about coaching. These programs may serve several purposes— for example, to introduce the subject of coaching, provide an overview of coaching skills training, reinforce some specific idea people may have been previously exposed to, and extend learning gained from earlier training sessions.

5. Half-Day Coaching Program

It is possible to conduct coaching skills training over an extended period of time divided into one- or half-day training sessions. The three-day design described in Chapter 8, for example, can be broken down into a series of smaller training sessions, that is, one- and half-day programs. Also, it is possible that you may want to give people only an extended introduction to coaching; a half-day program could serve that purpose. In addition, half-day programs can be used to reinforce previous learning and give participants additional skill practice in some aspect of coaching not previously covered.

6. One-Day Coaching Workshop

This chapter describes everything needed to deliver a one-day coaching skills training program. A one-day design can be a self-contained program that makes no assumptions about previous programs or those to follow. As with the half-day program, you may use the one-day program to deliver the more ambitious two- and three-day programs by breaking the longer programs into one-day sessions, offered over a period of time.

7. Two-Day Coaching Workshop

The two-day design permits participants to do more than just learn about coaching and the Superior Coaching Model. They are involved in many skill building exercises, and on the second day participate in two videotaped practice interactions. The two-day design provides a good foundation in coaching skills, and participants can be offered additional training at a later date.

8. Three-Day Coaching Workshop

This is the most ambitious program described in the sourcebook, providing participants with a solid foundation in the understanding and skills required to function as highly effective coaches. In this program, participants receive a solid grounding in the Superior Coaching Model and have time to obtain extensive feedback as they learn to use the major coaching functions.

9. Learning Activities

There are three sections in this chapter—Exercises, Learning Transfer Tools, and Program Evaluation Forms. All the exercises require participation and interaction. Since the most powerful tool we have for teaching new communication behaviors to people is video, we have included learning activities that make extensive use of videotaping and feedback. In this chapter you also will find numerous ways to help ensure that participants learn and apply the coaching skills gained in your programs.

10. Assessment Tools

A very useful learning method is to help participants in a training program assess their own understanding and competencies related to the subject being covered. This section contains several assessment tools you may incorporate into your coaching training programs.

11. Overhead Transparencies

This chapter includes all overheads needed to conduct all programs. They can, of course, be made into other kinds of visual aids, such as flip charts or slides, and can be used as handouts or included as content in participant notebooks.

Workshop Building Blocks

In this sourcebook, you have all the building blocks needed to create your own coaching training programs. The following pages provide Subject/Reference matrices to help you select the building blocks that fit your objectives.

Directions

To choose the building blocks needed for your training program, follow the steps below:

1. To locate sourcebook material on a specific topic, go to Column A and find the row that lists the topic needed.

2. Refer to the cells in that row to find page references for information and materials on the topic.

Subject/Reference Matrix

A. Topic	B. Information	C. Program Scripts	D. Activities	E. Trainer's Notes	F. Overheads
1. Trainer Preparation and Planning	• Chapter 1 • Chapter 2 • Chapter 3	• Chapter 4 • Chapter 5 • Chapter 6 • Chapter 7 • Chapter 8			• Workshop Title and Trainer's Name (p. 289) • Changes in Management and Leadership Functions (p. 290) • Objectives for One-Hour Program: The Superior Coaching Model (p. 291) • Objectives for One-Hour Program: The Critical Skills of Superior Coaching (p. 292) • Objectives for Half-Day Program: Introduction to Superior Coaching (p. 293) • Objectives for One-Day Workshop (p. 294) • Objectives for Two-Day Workshop (p. 295) • Objectives for Three-Day Workshop (p. 296) • Half-Day Program Flow (p. 297) • One-Day Program Flow (p. 298) • Two-Day Program Flow (p. 299) • Three-Day Program Flow (p. 301) • Program Norms (p. 303)

Subject/Reference Matrix

A. Topic	B. Information	C. Program Scripts	D. Activities	E. Trainer's Notes	F. Overheads
2. Program Introductions and Overviews		• Chapter 4 • Chapter 5 • Chapter 6 • Chapter 7 • Chapter 8			• Workshop Title and Trainer's Name (p. 289) • Changes in Management and Leadership Functions (p. 290) • Objectives for One-Hour Program: The Superior Coaching Model (p. 291) • Objectives for One-Hour Program: The Critical Skills of Superior Coaching (p. 292) • Objectives for Half-Day Program: Introduction to Superior Coaching (p. 293) • Objectives for One-Day Workshop (p. 294) • Objectives for Two-Day Workshop (p. 295) • Objectives for Three-Day Workshop (p. 296) • Half-Day Program Flow (p. 297) • One-Day Program Flow (p. 298) • Two-Day Program Flow (p. 299) • Three-Day Program Flow (p. 301) • Program Norms (p. 303)

Subject/Reference Matrix

A. Topic	B. Information	C. Program Scripts	D. Activities	E. Trainer's Notes	F. Overheads
3. Importance of Coaching	• Chapter 1	• Chapter 6 • Chapter 7 • Chapter 8	• How the Jobs of Leading and Managing are Changing and Why (p. 179) • Why Coaching Is Becoming So Important (p. 181) • What Is Superior Coaching? (p. 183)	• How the Jobs of Leading and Managing are Changing and Why (p. 178) • Why Coaching Is Becoming So Important (p. 180) • What Is Superior Coaching? (p. 182)	• Why Coaching Is Becoming So Important (p. 304)
4. Meaning of Superior Coaching	• Chapter 2	• Chapter 6 • Chapter 7 • Chapter 8			• The Meaning of Superior Coaching (p. 305)

Subject/Reference Matrix

	A. Topic	B. Information	C. Program Scripts	D. Activities	E. Trainer's Notes	F. Overheads
5.	**Superior Coaching Model**	• Chapter 2	• Chapter 4 • Chapter 5 • Chapter 6 • Chapter 7 • Chapter 8	• Understanding the Superior Coaching Model (p. 185)	• Understanding the Superior Coaching Model (p. 184)	• The Superior Coaching Model (p. 306)
6.	**Key Values**	• Chapter 2	• Chapter 6 • Chapter 7 • Chapter 8	• What Superior Coaches Believe (p. 200) • Clarifying Key Values and Essential Characteristics (p. 187)	• What Superior Coaches Believe (p. 199) • Clarifying Key Values and Essential Characteristics (p. 186)	• What Superior Coaches Believe (p. 309)

Subject/Reference Matrix

A. Topic	B. Information	C. Program Scripts	D. Activities	E. Trainer's Notes	F. Overheads
7. Essential Characteristics	• Chapter 2	• Chapter 6 • Chapter 7 • Chapter 8	• Clarifying Key Values and Essential Characteristics (p. 187) • Testing Our Understanding of Creating Balance (p. 202) • Practicing Being Concrete (p. 204) • Practicing Developing Shared Responsibility (p. 206) • Testing Our Understanding of Creating Shape (The Core Conversation) (p. 209) • Testing Our Understanding of Communicating Respect (p. 213) • Practicing Communicating Respect (p. 217)	• Clarifying Key Values and Essential Characteristics (p. 186) • Testing Our Understanding of Creating Balance (p. 201) • Practicing Being Concrete (p. 203) • Practicing Developing Shared Responsibility (p. 205) • Testing Our Understanding of Creating Shape (The Core Conversation) (p. 208) • Testing Our Understanding of Communicating Respect (p. 212) • Practicing Communicating Respect (p. 216)	• Essential Characteristics (p. 311) • Meaning of Balance (p. 312) • Meaning of Being Concrete (p. 313) • Meaning of Respect (p. 314)

Subject/Reference Matrix

A. Topic	B. Information	C. Program Scripts	D. Activities	E. Trainer's Notes	F. Overheads
8. **Critical Skills**	• Chapter 2	• Chapter 6 • Chapter 7 • Chapter 8	• Clarifying Critical Skills (p. 191) • Practicing Attending and Inquiring (p. 219) • Practicing Reflecting (p. 222) • Practicing Attending, Inquiring, and Reflecting (pp. 225–226) • Practicing Affirmation (p. 228) • Clarifying the Core Conversation (p. 196) • Testing Our Understanding of Creating Shape (The Core Conversation) (p. 209)	• Clarifying Critical Skills (p. 190) • Practicing Attending and Inquiring (p. 218) • Practicing Reflecting (p. 221) • Practicing Attending, Inquiring, and Reflecting (p. 224) • Practicing Affirmation (p. 227) • Clarifying the Core Conversation (p. 195) • Testing Our Understanding of Creating Shape (The Core Conversation) (p. 208)	• Critical Skills (p. 315)

Subject/Reference Matrix

A. Topic	B. Information	C. Program Scripts	D. Activities	E. Trainer's Notes	F. Overheads
9. Core Conversation	• Chapter 2	• Chapter 7 • Chapter 8	• Clarifying the Core Conversation (p. 196) • Testing Our Understanding of Creating Shape (The Core Conversation) (p. 209)	• Clarifying the Core Conversation (p. 195) • Testing Our Understanding of Creating Shape (The Core Conversation) (p. 208)	• The Core Conversation (p. 307)
10. Performance Applications	• Chapter 2	• Chapter 7 • Chapter 8	• Clarifying Performance Applications (p. 198) • Practice Interaction—Performance Application: Resolving Problems (pp. 232-237) • Practice Interaction—Performance Application: Teaching (pp. 239-243) • Practice Interaction—Performance Application: Supporting Performance (pp. 245-251) • Practice Interaction—Performance Application: Adjusting Performance (pp. 254-260)	• Clarifying Performance Applications (p. 197) • Practice Interaction—Performance Application: Resolving Problems (p. 231) • Practice Interaction—Performance Application: Teaching (p. 238) • Practice Interaction—Performance Application: Supporting Performance (p. 244) • Practice Interaction—Performance Application: Adjusting Performance (pp. 252-253)	• The Four Performance Applications (p. 308) • Resolving Problems Applications (p. 316) • Teaching Performance Application (p. 318) • Supporting Performance Application (p. 320) • Adjusting Performance Application (p. 322)

Subject/Reference Matrix

A. Topic	B. Information	C. Program Scripts	D. Activities	E. Trainer's Notes	F. Overheads
11. **Learning Transfer Tools**	• Chapter 9	• Chapter 7 • Chapter 8	• Review and Action Log (p. 263) • Review and Action Teams (p. 265) • Buddy System (p. 267) • Self Mail (p. 269) • Debriefings to Management (p. 271)	• Learning Transfer Tools (p. 261) • Review and Action Log (p. 262) • Review and Action Teams (p. 264) • Buddy System (p. 266) • Self Mail (p. 268) • Debriefings to Management (p. 270)	• Review and Action Teams (p. 324)
12. **Program Evaluation**	• Workshop Evaluation Forms (p. 272-276)	• Chapter 4 • Chapter 5 • Chapter 6 • Chapter 7 • Chapter 8	• Workshop Evaluation—Short Form (p. 273) • Workshop Evaluation—Long Form (pp. 275-276)	• Workshop Evaluation—Short Form (p. 272) • Workshop Evaluation—Long Form (p. 274)	

Subject/Reference Matrix

A. Topic	B. Information	C. Program Scripts	D. Activities	E. Trainer's Notes	F. Overheads
13. Assessment Tools	• Chapter 10		• Coaching Behavior Analysis (p. 279) • Coaching Values Questionnaire (p. 281) • Coaching Skills Feedback Questionnaire (p. 282)	• Using the CBA (Coaching Behavior Analysis) (p. 278) • Coaching Values Questionnaire (p. 281) • Coaching Skills Feedback Questionnaire (p. 282) • The Follow-Up Interview (p. 284) • The Follow-Up Questionnaire (p. 285) • Pre- and Post-Workshop Videotaping (p. 286)	

Navigating the Training Plans

The training plans are the heart of each of the seminar and work-shop sessions. These training plans are set out in detail on a module-by-module basis, with an agenda, statement of purpose, and objectives for each module. We have attempted to make these training plans as easy to use and as complete as possible. The icons are translated on the next page and a sample with annotations is on page 17.

1. Each section within a module has a heading that includes a statement of purpose for the section and suggested timing.

2. Within each section, you will find one or more major activities, each marked by an icon and a descriptive heading.

3. Additionally, you will find a number of supporting activities, each marked with an icon and explained with a suggested action.

4. Suggested actions are shown in conjunction with supporting activities, with the appropriate action verb in *UPPERCASE BOLD ITALIC*.

5. Suggested comments accompany many of the suggested actions. While these comments are fully "scripted," it is not intended that you "parrot" these remarks—but rather paraphrase the key thoughts in a way that is meaningful to you and the participants.

Understanding the Icons

Major activities   The following icons mark major activities:

 Activities that feature facilitator commentary. In these activities, you—as facilitator—present information that will be key to subsequent workshop activities.

 Activities carried out in table groups. You assign participants to small groups to complete the activity at hand.

 Activities that revolve around total training group discussion. Such activities typically follow major exercises on which participants have worked individually or in groups. This icon is also used as a signal to listen for specific comments.

Supporting activities   The following icons mark supporting activities:

 An overhead transparency is to be shown. The title of the overhead transparency is referenced in the text accompanying the icon.

 A prepared video for interactive presentations is to be used with video-ready equipment.

 A participant handout, part or all of a learning activity, or an assessment is to be handed out.

 A question is to be asked. Wording for the question is provided, as are suggested answers when appropriate.

 A flipchart is to be used. If the flipchart is one of the "prepared flipcharts" recommended for the workshop, its title will appear in the accompanying text.

 Denotes a conversation, dialog, or interaction between the coach and another person.

 Denotes the expanding phase of a coaching conversation.

 Denotes the focusing phase of a coaching conversation.

Notes   The following icons mark notes to the facilitator:

 Indicates a special note or suggested pre-work.

 Indicates when to call time for timed exercises.

 Marks the end of an exercise or section.

Sample Page

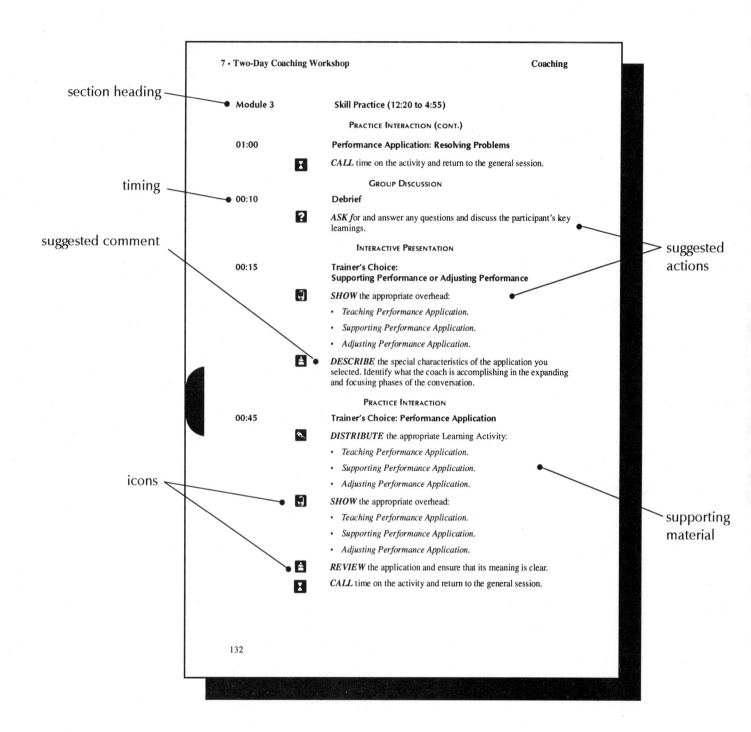

section heading

timing

suggested comment

icons

suggested actions

supporting material

---

7 · Two-Day Coaching Workshop   Coaching

Module 3   Skill Practice (12:20 to 4:55)

PRACTICE INTERACTION (CONT.)

01:00   **Performance Application: Resolving Problems**

CALL time on the activity and return to the general session.

GROUP DISCUSSION

00:10   **Debrief**

ASK for and answer any questions and discuss the participant's key learnings.

INTERACTIVE PRESENTATION

00:15   **Trainer's Choice:**
Supporting Performance or Adjusting Performance

SHOW the appropriate overhead:

• *Teaching Performance Application.*

• *Supporting Performance Application.*

• *Adjusting Performance Application.*

DESCRIBE the special characteristics of the application you selected. Identify what the coach is accomplishing in the expanding and focusing phases of the conversation.

PRACTICE INTERACTION

00:45   **Trainer's Choice: Performance Application**

DISTRIBUTE the appropriate Learning Activity:

• *Teaching Performance Application.*

• *Supporting Performance Application.*

• *Adjusting Performance Application.*

SHOW the appropriate overhead:

• *Teaching Performance Application.*

• *Supporting Performance Application.*

• *Adjusting Performance Application.*

REVIEW the application and ensure that its meaning is clear.

CALL time on the activity and return to the general session.

132

Chapter Two

Background

Anyone can presume to coach. Anyone can initiate conversations with their coworkers, even if they have only the vaguest idea of what they are trying to achieve without any clearly articulated understanding of how to conduct the coaching conversation. The results of such conversations will be random and unequal. By chance, anyone will, now and again conduct a conversation that achieves some useful results, like learning, understanding, and higher levels of commitment to superior performance.

Coaching training should remove, as much as possible, the element of chance from coaching conversations. For this to happen, coaching training must equip participants with a clear picture of just what a superior coaching conversation is and give them the critical skills required to conduct a superior coaching conversation.

Coaching is too important to be used without serious preparation and skill development because it carries so much potential to help individuals and teams achieve superior performance.

Coaching is a serious mental activity, and it requires extensive skill development. Coaching largely fails to impact on performance because people who try to coach have not developed a clear picture in their minds of just what a superior coaching conversation is, i.e., what are its essential characteristics and its flow or shape.

INTRODUCTION

This chapter prepares trainers for their job of designing and conducting coaching training by giving them a conceptual framework upon which they can build their programs. This framework consists of two primary elements:

- The Definition of Superior Coaching.

- The Superior Coaching Model.

Also included in this chapter is a glossary of key terms used in the sourcebook.

The Definition of Superior Coaching

Coaching is not a technical word and in common parlance has a variety of meanings (Kinlaw 1989). The more precisely coaching is defined, the more concrete our training programs and the more exact the skills taught will be.

The first step in designing and delivering a successful coaching training program is to decide, as carefully as possible, what we mean by coaching. But it is not just coaching that we are interested in any more than we are interested in team development. As far as team development is concerned, we should be interested in *superior* team development. As far as coaching is concerned, we are interested in *superior* coaching. What we will now do is develop a set of statements that we will use as building blocks to construct the meaning of superior coaching. We have used this definition in designing the programs and learning activities contained in this sourcebook. The place to start is the same place we should start with teaching, i.e., with results.

Results-oriented teaching affirms that unless there is learning, there is no teaching. If we apply this analogue to coaching, the very first thing we can say about coaching is that it is an activity that improves performance. It is, however, more than an activity that results in a single instance of improved performance; it is an activity that can lead to the continuous improvement of performance.

1. First Characteristic

Here, then, is a beginning definition of superior coaching that includes this first characteristic:

> Superior coaching is an activity that results in the continuous improvement of performance.

Most of what is done by managers, of course, should result in the continuous improvement of performance. Superior coaching is more specific. It is a conversation that involves at least two people, but may involve more. It may take place between a leader and one other person, or it may take place between a leader and a team. Incidentally, we will use the term "leader" throughout this sourcebook for anyone who assumes the leadership role of being a coach.

2.   Second Characteristic

When we add the second characteristic, conversation, to the first, we have enlarged our definition of coaching to be:

> Superior coaching is a conversation between a leader and an individual or a team that results in the continuous improvement of performance.

Therefore, superior coaching is a results-oriented activity. Like the teaching/learning analogy, the underlying assumption is that no coaching has taken place unless some positive change has resulted. Managers and leaders can have all kinds of conversations in which they attempt to improve some aspect of individual or team performance. But if no improvement occurs, then what did occur was an interaction of some kind, but not a coaching interaction, and certainly not a superior coaching interaction.

3.   Third Characteristic

So far, our definition of superior coaching has not described how to conduct coaching transactions to improve the probability of achieving positive results. Nor has it addressed the goal of achieving continuous improvement of performance. Superior coaching is *disciplined*. An exact definition of disciplined is explained in the next section on the Superior Coaching Model, which describes in detail the skills required of managers and leaders.

> Superior coaching is a disciplined conversation, using concrete performance information, between a leader and an individual or a team that results in the continuous improvement of performance.

Now that we have a solid description of superior coaching, we can look at the Superior Coaching Model, which translates this definition into specific elements that can, in turn, be used to design coaching training.

The Superior Coaching Model

The Superior Coaching Model is a functional, not theoretical, model. A functional model is one derived from empirical research—from hundreds of observations of coaching transactions, and from the experience of teaching thousands of managers and leaders how to coach. The model not only describes the ideal *elements* that should be present in a coaching interaction, but also describes what is typically present in every superior coaching interaction. The model describes qualitative aspects of superior coaching, and defines how coaching can be successfully applied to ensure the continuous improvement of performance.

The model defines exactly what a person must understand and do to be a superior coach and conveys the following:

 Results

Coaching is a results-oriented process that leads to the continuous improvement of performance.

 Discipline

Coaching is a disciplined interaction. To hit the target of continuous improvement, a coach must be disciplined enough to create the *essential characteristics*, develop and use the *critical skills*, and apply the *core coaching conversation.*

 Training

Superior coaching requires training.

 Values

Coaching begins with the coach and his/her *values*. It does not begin with learning a few behavioral tricks or clever communication ploys.

The model does not describe coaching—it describes *superior* coaching, i.e., coaching that has the highest probability of leading to the continuous improvement of performance.

Elements of the Superior Coaching Model

The Superior Coaching Model has the following elements:

- Key Values.

- Essential Characteristics.

- Critical Skills.

- Core Conversation.

- Performance Applications.

Each of these five elements of the Superior Coaching Model will be discussed in the following section.

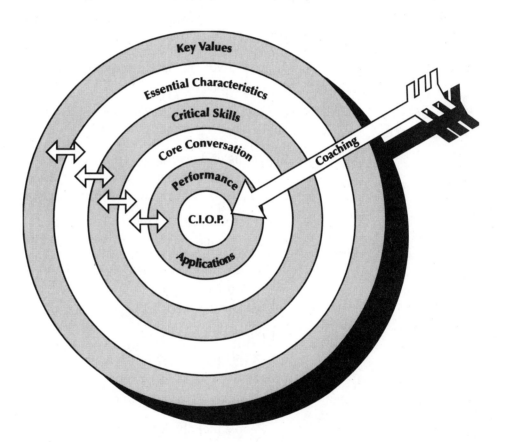

C.I.O.P. = Continuous Improvement of Performance

Key Values

Superior coaches are managers and leaders who share beliefs about:

- Human competency.

- Superior performance.

- Values of coaching.

These beliefs foster the knowledge that leads them to believe superior coaching to be one of the most important functions of managers and leaders.

Human competency

Superior coaches believe that people:

- Want to be competent, and, given the necessary help, will strive to become more competent.

- Must be given the opportunity to demonstrate their competency on a continual basis.

Superior performance

Superior coaches share a commitment to superior performance, believing that:

- Managing and leading by control is not practical and does not lead to a commitment to superior performance or the continuous improvement of superior performance.

- Superior performance results from the commitment of individuals and teams to perform at the best of their ability.

Such commitment is a function of at least the following conditions:

- People understand what they are doing and why it is important.

- People have the competencies to perform the jobs that are expected of them.

- People feel appreciated for what they do.

- People feel challenged by their jobs.

- People have the chance to improve when they make mistakes.

Values of coaching

Superior coaches hold common values about the importance of coaching. They also share key values about how to coach, i.e., their understanding of coaching and the way they actually interact with people in their coaching conversations.

Superior coaches believe:

- That they must initiate coaching interactions and use every interaction with individuals and teams as a potential opportunity to coach—rather than to direct.

- In discipline, and view coaching as a set of competencies that can be learned and tested like any other set of skills required for managing and leading.

One of the first and very important sets of activities in the longer coaching program plans described in Chapters 5 through 8 helps participants understand what they currently believe about coaching and how their beliefs influence the way they initiate and use coaching.

Essential Characteristics

Positive results from coaching interactions depend on the following:

- The coach creates essential conditions that support superior coaching.

- The coach employs the critical skills for superior coaching.

- The coach is disciplined enough to create the structure of the core coaching conversation which underlies superior coaching.

- The coach is able to apply the skills and core conversation to specific opportunities for continuous improvement of performance.

The logic is that the superior coach moves from his/her internal set of values into learning all that it takes to be a superior coach, i.e.: creating the essential characteristics, learning to use the critical skills, learning to use the skills to create the core conversation, and then applying all this to various performance applications.

Characteristics describe the qualities that distinguish a superior coaching conversation from other such conversations. Characteristics describe the concrete and verifiable differences between superior coaching conversations and other conversations.

Five essential characteristics

Five characteristics distinguish a superior coaching conversation from other conversations. Superior coaches use disciplined behavior and aim to create it in others by example. Look for the following specific qualities of superior coaching.

1. Balance

Superior coaching is not one-sided. There is give and take, a questioning and sharing of information and ideas with the full involvement of all parties. A superior coach creates balance through skilled and disciplined behavior. In some conversations the coach will do most of the initiating, but in others, it will be the persons being coached.

2. Being Concrete

Another characteristic of superior coaching is that it focuses on what can be improved. The coach uses language that is to the point and encourages the persons being coached to be specific. It focuses on the objective and descriptive aspects of performance. Performance can be improved only when it can be described so precisely that both coach and those being coached understand what is being discussed. It is pointless to try to help someone be, for example, more conscientious or a better team player, unless we have defined our expectations so clearly that there is no doubt what we are talking about. When, for instance, the training programs use exercises that teach a skill, that skill is described as behavior so that it can be observed and verified.

3. Shared Responsibility

Both the coach and the persons being coached have a shared responsibility to work together for the continuous improvement of performance. All participants in a coaching conversation share the responsibility for making that conversation as useful as possible, and for the continuous improvement of performance that follows the conversation.

4. Shape

Superior coaching has a distinctive shape that can be reproduced over and over again. The shape is determined by these important factors:

- The goal of the coaching conversation is clearly stated.

- The flow of the conversation expands information and then focuses the information as the participants move toward the goal.

The idea of shape is introduced here as a characteristic. Like all characteristics, it is created by skilled behavior.

The meaning of shape becomes quite explicit when we discuss the core conversation. We have made the core conversation a separate element in the Superior Coaching Model to emphasize its importance. Think of it this way: the shape of the conversation reflects the dynamics of superior coaching. We will discuss more about the skills needed to shape a conversation when we look at the core conversation. The core conversation is the shape that is characteristic of superior coaching conversations. It is the core conversation which is the foundation shape of all superior coaching interactions.

5. Respect

A final qualitative characteristic of superior coaching is that the leader communicates respect for the people being coached. Demonstrating respect uses behaviors in a conversation which involve the other person and make that person a fully accepted player.

We have now looked at the first two elements in the Superior Coaching Model—key values and essential characteristics. The logic of learning how to be a superior coach is the same logic you will find underlying each of the longer training designs in Chapters 5 through 8. Each design starts with the Superior Coaching Model and then proceeds through each element in the model.

Critical Skills

To act on their values, superior coaches must translate their understanding of superior coaching into behavior. Superior coaches have the following skills for interacting with others:

- Attending.
- Inquiring.
- Reflecting.
- Affirming.
- Being disciplined.

Keep in mind the following as you become familiar with these skills and begin to think about teaching them to others: the purpose of these skills is to demonstrate the essential characteristics of the superior coaching conversation in every performance application.

These skills are not, however, all the skills required for superior coaching—each coaching application may require the use of additional skills. (Chapter 8 describes coaching applications that use some of these special skills.)

Attending

The term *attending* refers to what coaches do to convey they are listening. There is a vocal and nonvocal element in attending. The nonvocal element includes such behaviors as:

- Facing the other person.
- Keeping comfortable eye contact.
- Nodding in agreement.
- Avoiding distracting behaviors such as fidgeting, thumbing through papers, and interrupting.

The vocal aspects of attending include all the grunts and groans that communicate to the other person that the coach is paying attention. These vocal behaviors include such responses as "uh huh," "yes," "I can see that," "ok," and the like.

The nonvocal aspects of attending do not ensure that the coach is actually listening. These behaviors have the effect of conveying to the other person that the coach is listening and, therefore, encourage the other person to interact easily and to develop necessary information.

Attending behaviors also have an effect on the coach. Attending helps discipline the coach to listen. These behaviors facilitate the coach's concentration on what the other person is communicating.

The key to listening to the other person is first to focus one's eyes, ears, and mind on what the other person is communicating. There is, however, another important aspect of listening to understand. This is the ability to suspend judgment—the ability to listen without immediately taking sides. It means working at understanding what the other person is trying to communicate rather than deciding if what the person is communicating is right or wrong, or if you agree with it or not.

When coaches make premature judgments they disrupt the development of information and communicate a lack of respect for the other person, which destroys the shape of the superior coaching conversation. They do this by:

- Being too quick to reject what the other person is trying to communicate.

- Being too quick to use their own beliefs and values to interpret what the other person is trying to communicate.

- Thinking too much about what they want to say, rather than hearing what the other person is trying to say.

- Being too quick to give irrelevant information not needed by the other person or not needed to resolve the problem being discussed.

Inquiring

The second critical skill is inquiring. Another key to superior coaching is to develop sufficient information so positive results can be achieved. The information base for coaching is one of the distinguishing characteristics of superior coaching. Coaches can teach others by knowing what the other persons need to know. Coaches can help others resolve problems by knowing how other persons understand the problem, what they have done to resolve it, and how they think it should be resolved.

Inquiring takes the following forms:

- **Questions**

  "So what did you do when you learned the contractor was going to be late completing the first phase?"

- **Directives**

  "Tell me what you did when you learned the contractor was going to be late completing the first phase."

Questions and directives may be closed or open. A closed question might be, "Should Jones be included on the team?" An open question might be, "What sort of people do you think we should put on the team?" A closed directive might be, "Tell me how long it will take for you to complete the plan." An open directive might be, "Tell me what you think you must do to complete the plan."

Attending and inquiring are both behaviors that help the coach learn the information required to conduct a superior coaching conversation.

Reflecting

A third behavior that helps the coach develop information is *reflecting*. Reflecting is a behavior by which coaches communicate that they:

- Are listening.

- Understand what the other person is saying and/or feeling.

- Have suspended judgment.

- Want the other person to develop information that is important to that person.

Reflecting is not mirroring or repeating verbatim what the other person has said. It is playing back to the other person what the coach believes has been said, and/or communicating the feelings that the other person has conveyed as shown in the following examples:

Other: "It just isn't possible to get the contractor to respond. He has it in his head that he works for his corporate head-quarters and not for me."

Coach: "So, you feel almost powerless to get him to do the job you think he should."

Other: "I don't see how I can keep putting my people on all these *Total Quality Management* (T.Q.M.) teams. I have just enough people to manage our trouble calls. If they are all on teams, it's me that's going to get the flak when somebody has a computer down. My customers don't care about my problems."

Coach: "The way you see it at the moment is that you're in a no-win situation. Management wants you to participate in its T.Q.M. program, but to you that means you may disappoint your customers."

Other: "I don't see how the company can expect me to bust my buns when I know that the more I do, the more I get to do. There is no chance for promotion and our bonus system is a joke."

Coach: "I guess the big issue for you is that you don't feel properly rewarded or valued because of what you do."

Affirming

The first three critical skills tend to create the essential characteristics of balance, shared responsibility, and respect. They are skills which also shape the conversation by developing information with the other person. The fourth critical skill is affirming, which focuses on the final outcome of coaching—the continuous improvement of performance. Affirming puts into direct action the coach's belief that people want to be competent. Affirming reinforces the sense of competency in the other person and contributes directly to that person's commitment to continuous improvement.

Affirming during a coaching interaction may draw attention to two sets of competencies that the other person has demonstrated: first, those competencies which the person has demonstrated on the job; second, those competencies that the person demonstrates during a coaching interaction. In the examples below, we have related each example to one of the coaching applications that will be discussed later under the heading, Performance Applications (p. 34). When you get to that section, we suggest that you come back and look at these examples again.

- **Teaching**

   "I know it was tough for you to spend so much time learning the new accounting system, and I know it hasn't been easy having these sessions with me to help you get up to speed in a hurry. You have really done a fine job."

- **Resolving Problems**

   "Thanks for the way you've tried to resolve this problem with your team. It has been very helpful to me to understand better just what issues you all face. Most of all, I appreciate your candor and your willingness to keep me informed. I know that it isn't always easy to resolve problems like this."

- **Supporting Performance**

   "Getting those movers lined up the way you did was exactly what we needed to get into our new spaces on time. I have some idea of how much time you had to spend on this, but it was a major help in getting us moved with as little down time as we had. You were a great help."

- **Adjusting Performance**

   "I think we really got somewhere today. I feel now that this kind of problem has been fixed once and for all. There is absolutely no reason now that you can't stay on track and be one of our best team members."

Being disciplined

The last critical skill is *being disciplined*. This is not so much a specific skill as it is the ability to use the other four skills—attending, inquiring, reflecting and affirming—to create the essential characteristics of superior coaching.

Being disciplined means, at the least:

- Assuming responsibility for one's own behavior and accepting the responsibility for the outcome of a coaching interaction. It is the clearheaded and responsible approach which says, "If it didn't turn out so well, I had something to do with it," and "If it did turn out well, I had something to do with it."

- Understanding and being committed to creating the essential characteristics of superior coaching during every coaching interaction.

- Understanding and being committed to creating the general shape of every superior coaching conversation.

Being disciplined starts with the definition of superior coaching:

> Coaching is a disciplined conversation, using concrete performance information, that takes place between a leader and an individual or a team that results in the continuous improvement of performance.

Disciplined coaches feel responsible for the outcome of their coaching conversations in the same way that athletic coaches feel responsible for the outcome of their teams' contests. Disciplined coaches always look first to themselves to learn why their coaching conversations are not working and why they are not achieving the desired level of improved performance.

Discipline next requires a thorough understanding of the Superior Coaching Model. It means understanding that coaching is not a random event. Coaching is a disciplined interaction that depends on the personal discipline of the coach.

Core Conversation

One aspect of being disciplined that we have referred to but not yet developed is the disciplined use of the core conversation. This section describes the core conversation and how it relates to the other elements in the Superior Coaching Model.

Being disciplined means to employ the Superior Coaching Model in every coaching interaction. One characteristic of superior coaching is that it has shape. The specific meaning of shape is that the shape of a superior coaching conversation looks like the core conversation. A major aspect of being disciplined is the ability to create the shape of the core conversation.

This figure illustrates the simple, two-phased structure that underlies most coaching conversations. The core conversation is a process of expanding upon and then focusing in on information.

In the first phase the coach does two things:

1. Gives the other person what information the coach has relative to the purpose of the interaction.

2. Assists the other person to develop relative information.

In the second phase of the core conversation the coach applies the information from the first phase to achieve a positive result.

The core conversation represents the general flow or logical progress of a superior coaching interaction. The core conversation, of course, only exists within some specific performance application. In the next section we will describe the major ways to apply the core conversation.

Performance Applications

Each performance application described below includes examples of how the core conversation might look and ideas of what a superior coach might accomplish in the two phases of the core conversation:

- Resolving problems.

- Teaching.

- Supporting performance.

- Adjusting performance.

Resolving problems

The first performance application of coaching includes the many kinds of conversations in which managers and leaders work to resolve a wide variety of problems presented to them by others. The problems may be technical; they may relate to schedules or organizational relationships; they may pertain to careers; they may be personal. Using the core conversation to chart what should be happening in a conversation to resolve problems, look for specific events in each of the two phases.

Expanding Phase

In the expanding phase of a problem solving interaction the coach will develop information that leads to a mutual understanding of:

- The problem or problems.

- The history of the problem.

- The cause(s) of the problem.

- The implications if the problem is not resolved.

Focusing Phase

In the focusing phase of a problem solving interaction the coach will use information developed in the expanding phase to mutually:

- Develop alternative strategies for resolving the problem.

- Agree on a plan to resolve the problem.

- Agree on a follow-up plan to track progress.

Teaching

Teaching is another primary function of coaches, who may teach individuals and teams technical information and skills and the values and culture of the organization—sometimes called mentoring. Coaches use the process of personal interaction to increase the competencies of individuals and teams. When we apply the core conversation to teaching, we can see what the superior coach is conscious of trying to achieve in each phase of the conversation.

Expanding Phase

In the expanding phase of a teaching interaction the coach will develop information that leads to a mutual understanding of:

- What the coach wants the other person to learn, i.e., the goals of the conversation.
- What the other person already knows.
- How the conversation will proceed, i.e., the sequence.

Focusing Phase

In the focusing phase of the interaction the coach will use the information developed in the expanding phase to:

- Teach the content that the other person needs to learn.
- Request feedback or a demonstration to ensure that learning has occurred.
- Clear up any residual questions the other person might have.

Supporting performance

In addition to resolving problems and teaching, coaches also interact with individuals and teams to support their performance. Supporting performance can mean giving information about changes in requirements or expectations, or giving feedback to assure others that their performance is on target, or expressing appreciation for the performance of others.

Expanding Phase

In the expanding phase of a coaching interaction to support performance the coach will develop information that leads to a:

- Clear description of the performance being discussed.
- Clarification of expectations concerning the performance.
- Mutual understanding of the importance of the performance.

Focusing Phase

In the focusing phase of this interaction the coach will use the information developed in the expanding phase to:

- Give feedback about the performance.
- Express mutual agreement about changes in performance requirements or expectations.
- Express appreciation for the performance.

Adjusting performance

Sometimes coaches must make significant adjustments in the performance of individuals and teams. They must confront performance that is below expectations or established standards, and also challenge people who are performing at one level to move to a higher level, i.e., people who should be taking on more difficult tasks and assignments. When we apply the core conversation to adjusting performance we can expect the following kinds of things to be achieved in each phase.

Expanding Phase

In the expanding phase of a coaching interaction to adjust performance the coach will develop information that leads to:

- Identification of the specific performance being discussed.

- A concrete statement of what the coach believes to be the problem in performance.

- The other person's understanding of the problem.

- An agreement concerning the nature of the performance problem.

- Clarity about who is responsible for resolving the problem.

- Alternative strategies for resolving the problem.

Focusing Phase

In the focusing phase of this interaction the coach will use the information developed in the expanding phase to accomplish mutual agreement about:

- Which performance will be adjusted and to what degree.

- A plan to adjust performance.

- A follow-up plan to monitor progress.

Review of the Superior Coaching Model

We have now looked at each element in the Superior Coaching Model. It is important, not only to know the elements of the model and what they mean, but also to keep in mind just how these elements are interrelated. The key points to remember are:

1. The model, first of all, emphasizes that coaching is a results-oriented process. The bull's eye of the model represents continuous improvement of performance (C.I.O.P.). There has been no coaching unless performance has been improved.

2. The model is a graphic description of the definition of superior coaching:

> **SUPERIOR COACHING**
>
> Superior coaching is a disciplined conversation, using concrete performance information, that takes place between a leader and an individual or a team that results in the continuous improvement of performance.

What makes the conversation disciplined is that the coach proceeds through each of the rings in the model—from his/her values, to essential characteristics, to critical skills, to core conversation, and on to applications.

3. The model describes exactly what the superior coach must be able to do. The superior coach creates the essential characteristics of balance, being concrete, shared responsibility, shape, and respect.

4. The model communicates that the superior coach is competent in using the critical skills of attending, inquiring, reflecting, affirming, and being disciplined.

5. The model indicates that the superior coach understands the core conversation which provides the underlying structure for superior coaching interactions. The superior coach enters each coaching interaction with the expectation to *expand* the conversation to include all the information needed to achieve the purpose of the conversation, and to *focus* this information to achieve the purpose, i.e., teach, resolve a problem, etc.

6. The model provides a clear description of the major performance applications: teaching, resolving problems, supporting performance, and adjusting performance.

How the Model Is Used In This Sourcebook

The Superior Coaching Model provides the conceptual basis and structure for designing coaching skills programs and for developing all materials that go into those programs. It relates to the program training plans, exercises, and other materials in the following ways.

1. The model is used to give trainers a clear frame of reference for understanding coaching and what might be included in a coaching skills training program.

2. The model is used as a concrete and graphic tool for communicating to program participants the meaning of coaching and what it takes to become a superior coach.

3. Third, the model not only provides a logical description of the sequential steps for becoming a superior coach, but this same sequence is used for training people to be superior coaches.

4. Fourth, the elements in the model provide the actual topics for coaching skills training programs.

In the training plans that follow, the elements in the model will become segments in each training sequence.

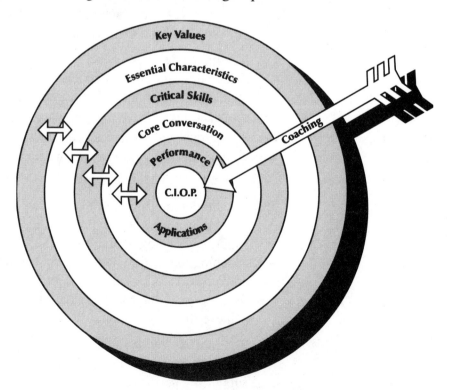

C.I.O.P. = Continuous Improvement of Performance

Key Terms

Affirming	Fourth critical skill. This occurs when the coach reinforces the sense of competency in people being trained and contributes to their commitment to continuous improvement.
Attending	First critical skill. Vocal and nonvocal behaviors that coaches use to convey that they are listening.
Balance	First essential characteristic. The give and take created by a superior coach during a coaching interaction that ensures full participation of the other person or team.
Behavior Model	Live or videotaped interaction that demonstrates the exact behavioral skills that trainees are to practice and learn.
Behavior Modeling	Process of using interactive demonstrations that illustrate the exact behavioral skills that trainees are to practice and learn.
Being Disciplined	Fifth critical skill. The ability to use the other four skills—attending, inquiring, reflecting and affirming—to create the essential characteristics of superior coaching.
Coaching Interaction	Formal and informal conversations between coaches and individuals or teams which are focused on improving performance.
Concrete	Language used by coaches that focuses on the objective and descriptive aspects of performance and leads to a mutual understanding of what is being discussed.

Core Conversation	Fourth element in the Superior Coaching Model. Shape of a superior coaching conversation. Foundation shape of all superior coaching interactions. Represents the general flow or logical progress of a superior coaching interaction.
Critical Skills	Third element in the Superior Coaching Model. Skills that superior coaches use when conducting coaching interactions: attending, inquiring, reflecting, affirming, and being disciplined.
Debrief	Activities at the end of an exercise for participants to report results of an activity and the facilitator to sum up key learnings.
Discipline	A critical skill. The ability to use all the skills required for a superior coaching interaction.
Element	One part of the Superior Coaching Model.
Essential Characteristics	Second element in the Superior Coaching Model. Describes one of the concrete and verifiable differences between superior coaching conversations and other conversations. Essential characteristics are balance, being concrete, shared responsibility, shape, and respect.
Expanding Phase	First phase of the core conversation in which the coach focuses on clarifying the purpose of the coaching interaction and developing information.
Extended Interaction	Exercise in which trainees practice using all or a portion of the Superior Coaching Model.
Focusing Phase	Second phase of the core conversation in which the coach focuses on achieving the purposes of the conversation, i.e., resolving a problem, teaching a skill, supporting performance, adjusting performance.

Human Competency	First key value. Superior coaches believe that people want to be competent, and given the opportunity, will strive to become more competent.
Inquiring	Second critical skill used by superior coaches. Questions and directives that can be open or closed.
Interactive Presentation	Presentation by facilitator which fully involves participants by asking for their comments and questions.
Key Values	First element in the Superior Coaching Model. Beliefs superior coaches hold about human competency, how people committed to superior performance are developed, the value of coaching.
Performance Applications	Fifth element in the Superior Coaching Model. Describes the ways coaching is applied to improve performance: resolving problems, teaching new knowledge or skills, supporting performance, adjusting performance.
Reflecting	Third critical skill. Coach conveys understanding by playing back to the other person or team in the coach's own words what has been communicated by the other person or team.
Respect	Fifth essential characteristic. Demonstrated by avoiding behaviors that imply a person to be stupid, evil or inferior; conversation that involves the other person or team and makes that person or team fully accepted players.
Shape	Fourth essential characteristic. A characteristic of superior coaching conversations.
Shared Responsibility	Responsibility for the continuous improvement of performance which superior coaches create with the persons they coach.

Spaced Training	Training related to a single primary topic broken into segments or modules and delivered with days or weeks intervening between segments or modules.
Superior Coaching	Disciplined conversation, using concrete performance information, that takes place between a leader and an individual or team that results in the continuous improvement of performance.
Superior Coaching Conversation	Vocal and nonvocal elements in a coaching interaction that lead to the continuous improvement of performance.
Superior Coaching Interaction	Conversations and other elements included in the process of coaching individuals and teams.
Superior Coaching Model	Graphic representation of elements present in superior coaching interactions. The elements are key values, essential characteristics, critical skills, core conversation, performance applications.
Transition	Comments made by facilitator which make bridges or connections between one activity and another to help participants know where they are in the flow of a training program.
Value of Coaching	Third key value. Set of common values held by coaches concerning how to coach and interact with people in their coaching conversations.

Chapter Three:

Workshop Preparation

This is a sourcebook, not a cookbook. It is written with the assumption that those using it already have the basic tools for being trainers and have had some experience delivering training programs.

HOW TO USE THIS SOURCEBOOK

You can use this book in a variety of ways:

- The program designs may be presented with little or no modification.

- Trainers may use the learning activities and other materials to design their own programs.

- Trainers may use the materials to supplement the coaching skills training programs they are already delivering.

This sourcebook places emphasis on providing a conceptual basis for designing and delivering coaching skills training programs. Trainers will find a large resource of learning activities, assessment tools, visual aids, and ways to ensure the transfer of learning. The trainer's notes provided with the designs in Chapters 4 through 8 are not transcripts of training programs; rather, they define the materials to be used, how long each event in the program should take, and offer suggestions for making transitions from one event to another.

Becoming Familiar with the Materials

Experienced trainers will find their own way to plan and prepare for a coaching skills program. The following four steps will help you extract the greatest benefit from this book:

1. Become thoroughly familiar with this book and its contents. If you have not already done so, read the complete book before you begin to plan your programs. As you do this, keep a notebook and record questions and ideas for future use.

2. Once familiar with the material, reread Chapter 2. By that time, you should be able to:

   - Develop your own clear coaching rationale.

   - Understand the definition of superior coaching.

   - Describe in your own words the Superior Coaching Model.

   You must become so familiar with the Superior Coaching Model that you are able to draw the model from memory. Each design and exercise depends on the model. It is essential that you are able to describe the model, the meaning of each of its *elements*, and the relationship among the elements.

3. Once you are completely familiar with the Superior Coaching Model, you are ready to understand the designs in Chapters 4 through 8, and the learning activities in Chapter 8. As you read Chapters 4 through 8, look up the learning activities as they are referenced. Make certain you understand the objectives and content of each training plan, how they differ, and how the learning activities, overheads, and other materials are integrated into the plans. By following this process, you will soon have a thorough knowledge of the book's contents and know how all the chapters fit together.

   Although we have included descriptions of five different training plans, you may modify the designs to meet special training needs of your participants, to conform to the special constraints of your customers, and to capitalize on your own expertise and strengths. Making such modifications is quite easy, provided you have become thoroughly familiar with all materials.

4. Next, read carefully the entire set of learning activities in Chapter 9 noticing how each learning activity is structured. Pick out several learning activities, and find where they are used in the training plans. Then, understand the purpose of each learning activity and how each can be applied to achieve the specific goals of your training.

Introduction to the Training Designs

This section introduces you to the design and common elements of the training designs and workshops in Chapters 4 through 8.

Coaching training programs can be designed in an unlimited number of ways. Determine the length and content of a program by answering the following questions:

1. **Who is your target population?**

    Your students may never have been exposed to the concept of coaching or superior coaching, they may be experienced workshop participants who are returning for a refresher course, or some combination of the two.

2. **How much total coaching training do you intend to provide your target population?**

    Chapters 4 through 8 contain designs ranging from one hour to three days. It is only the two- and three-day designs which result in demonstrable skill acquisition. It may be necessary, however, for a variety of reasons, to deliver programs that last less than a full day. Because skill acquisition is a function of practice, feedback, correction, and more practice, programs that last less than two days—unless they are programs that extend or reinforce previous learning—will not produce skill acquisition. They can, of course, produce various levels of cognitive learning.

3. **Do you plan to use *spaced training* or *continuous training*?**

    Spaced training refers to training in which segments are separated in time. For example, a three-day coaching program could be delivered in three, one-day segments, or in one, two-day segment and a one-day segment. It is even possible to break up longer programs into half-day segments or any combination of day and half-day segments.

    The three-, two-, and one-day designs are complete programs, and participants should not need further coaching training. There can be, of course, more training, but these designs give a complete description of superior coaching. They differ in the amount of in-depth understanding participants receive and the number and variety of skill practice opportunities.

4. How large a group will you train?

The one-hour designs can be delivered to any number of people. The size and length of half-day sessions will be determined by the objectives of the design. If you are simply delivering information, then any number of people can attend; if you wish to reinforce some previously learned skill or teach a new skill, then the number of participants must be limited. The one-, two-, and three-day sessions are designed for groups of up to eighteen members. This provides three subgroups of six members each. If you exceed this number, you will need to modify the designs because each learning activity will take more time to complete.

5. Do you plan to use video to tape and replay the practice interaction exercises?

Videotaping and replay is the most powerful tool for improving interpersonal communication. We have, however, designed interaction exercises both with and without video. If you use video, you lengthen the time needed to complete a practice interaction exercise.

Program Elements

The one-, two-, and three-day training plans contain common elements. The half-day designs will contain some of these elements, but may not contain all—depending on the workshop objectives. The common elements are:

- Exercises.
- Exercise debriefs.
- Interactive presentations.
- Transitions.
- Reviews/previews.
- Review and action (R&A) teams.
- Learning transfer activities.
- Workshop evaluations.

The one-hour training plan typically incorporates only one or more of the following activities:

Exercises

The exercises in Chapter 9 are the foundation of the longer programs. They are designed to involve participants fully and help them assume responsibility for their own learning. They reinforce all *interactive presentations*, and are the means for skill practice and skill acquisition.

Exercise debriefs

Debriefs give participants time to report the results of the exercises and give you an opportunity to sum up key points. Suggestions about what should be covered in debriefs are included with each design.

Interactive presentations

Each coaching skills program is designed to involve participants fully in every aspect of the program. Interactive presentations ask participants to contribute their ideas and comments during every presentation. The exception, of course, may occur in one-hour programs given to very large groups.

To encourage interaction:

- Ask participants to interpret the information presented.
- Ask participants to share their experiences regarding a topic or point made.
- Ask participants what they would do in a similar situation.
- Encourage participants to add information and ideas to augment and enrich the presentation.

Suggestions for interactive presentations are provided with each training plan in Chapters 4 through 8. Chapter 11, Overhead Transparencies, contains the visual aids that support these presentations.

Transitions

Transitions between activities ensure that participants understand the main points covered. Suggestions for key points to cover in transitions are included with the designs. A transition serves the following purposes:

- To clarify the purpose of an activity.
- To connect an activity with those that precede and follow.
- To help participants know where they are at all times in the program's flow.
- To give the trainer an opportunity to summarize and reinforce key points.

Reviews/previews

Reviews and previews alert trainers to opportunities for summarizing key learning points at the end of a complete unit and for helping participants anticipate the next unit. The points to cover are outlined in Chapters 4 through 8. The overheads and charts provided in Chapter 11 are useful tools for making reviews and previews.

Review and action teams

In the two- and three-day programs, participants are organized into review and action (R&A) teams. There is not time in any of the shorter programs to use R&A teams, unless the one- and half-day programs are follow-up programs and the R&A teams were organized previously.

R&A teams meet throughout the programs at specified times to review their experience in the program, their key learning points, and to discuss their personal action plans. They use their R&A logs in these sessions. Details about these teams and the tools they use to apply their learning are found in Chapter 9.

If participants are attending the program with people from their own organization, they are expected to meet periodically with their R&A team to reinforce their learning and help team members continue to apply the knowledge and skills gained from the program. Team activity trainers give teams specific guidance for what they should accomplish.

Learning transfer tools

The goals of all training conducted in and for the organization are:

1. To transfer new knowledge and skills to the participants.

2. To help ensure that participants apply what they have learned to their jobs and work environment.

3. To improve the overall performance of the organization.

The tools that help participants transfer their learning are found in Chapter 8, Learning Activities. You will also find the following tools to help ensure that participants reinforce and apply what they have learned and to ensure that this knowledge begins to make a difference in their performance and that of their organizations:

- Review and Action Logs.

- The Buddy System.

- Self Mail.

- Participant Debriefs to Management.

Workshop evaluation

The final element in the training plan is workshop evaluation. Chapter 9 includes two forms, one for use with one-hour programs and one for use with the longer programs.

Workshop Agenda Template

Use this generic workshop agenda template to block out your programs and plan what methods and media to use.

Agenda	Topics, Key Points	Time Allotted	Start	Stop	Training Method	Media	Sourcebook Pages
1. Welcome							
2. Overview							
3. Learning Activity							
4. Debrief							
5. Break							
6. Interactive Presentation							
7. Debrief							
8. Lunch							
9. Interactive Presentation							
10. Learning Activity							
11. Debrief							
12. Review							
13. Evaluations							
14. Adjourn							

Using Videotaped Feedback Exercises

There are four practice interactions which give participants an opportunity to test and apply what they have learned to the following coaching interactions: resolving problems, teaching, supporting performance, and adjusting performance.

Video replay provides participants with a great deal of information. Videotaping and replay is the best tool that we have for teaching communication training to people. It is strongly recommended that trainers use the extended interaction exercises designed for videotaping and replay.

Follow these guidelines when using a videotaping and replay format:

1. Keep participants focused on the purpose of the exercises—which is to demonstrate the practical application of the Superior Coaching Model.

2. Encourage participants to use the observation sheets provided with each of the interaction exercises. The skills and behaviors described on the observation sheets help participants focus on relevant feedback.

3. Feedback should be balanced and emphasize the positive aspects of a participant's performance. Avoid giving participants too much negative feedback on the performance in the interaction exercises.

Video Behavior Models

One way to enrich your training program is to develop a set of video behavior models that illustrate the application of coaching to resolve problems, teach, support performance, and adjust performance. Use behavior models to demonstrate exactly what participants will be expected to do in their interactions. Develop one *behavior model* for each of the four extended interactions, and use the videotaped model before participants practice each interaction. Have participants record their comments on the observation sheets. There are two ways to do this:

• Collect examples from the programs you run. Most participants are quite willing to give you permission to use them as examples in later programs.

• Invite respected managers to participate in the development of the videotaped behavior models.

The advantage of using people with established reputation and position is obvious.

You do not need to develop a full script when you make video behavior models. In fact, it is always best to give the individuals who serve as behavior models scenarios they understand, and then let them apply the Superior Coaching Model and skills spontaneously and unrehearsed.

Now that you have a good idea about the contents of this sourcebook and how you can use it, you are ready to learn more about the meaning of coaching and how we will be using the term superior coaching throughout this book. These subjects are examined in the next chapter.

Trainer Preparation

Detailed and specific information about each workshop and its delivery are found in Chapters 4 through 8. All of the programs, though different in length and content, share a common requirement for trainer preparation and planning. Also, preceding each exercise in Chapter 9, Learning Activities, is a page of Trainer's Notes describing the exercise objectives, the time required, and the resources needed. Also included is an outline on how the exercise should be presented and debriefed.

When planning a coaching training program you must also make decisions about pre-program administration and materials you will use. If you plan to use video, refer to page 50.

Workshop Announcement

Prior to attending a coaching training program, participants should receive the following information about the workshop and what they must do to prepare for this session:

Program overview

Send each participant a brief description of the program, including schedule, content and benefits.

Location, date and time of training

Clearly state the date and time of the session and its location—and include a map to the training facility, if necessary.

Guidelines for appropriate clothing

Let participants know in advance if they are to wear business attire or casual dress.

Contact name and telephone number

Workshop Checklist

Program title: _____

Program date: _____ **Time:** _____

Name of facilitator: _____

Location: _____

Number of participants: _____

Materials Needed

Use the following checklist to make sure you have all the items needed for a successful program.

Training Setting and Facilities

☐ A meeting room large enough to accommodate participant teams.

☐ Separate tables for each team. All teams should have a clear view of overheads and charts presented by the trainer.

☐ A breakout room for each team, if needed.

☐ Tables for supplies.

☐ Extra seating for special guests or observers.

☐ Refreshment table (optional).

Materials and Supplies

☐ This sourcebook as a trainer's reference.

☐ Copies of all the participants' materials, one per person. It is a good idea to produce your own participant's workbooks from the materials in this book. There are handouts and, if you do not produce a workbook, then provide participants with a three-ring binder for filing and retaining program materials. Have a few extras of all materials just in case visitors or participants are added to the program at the last minute.

☐ Copies of Observation Sheets and interaction exercises.

☐ Copies of all the overheads to be used in the program, arranged in order of use.

☐ All charts to be used.

☐ Flip chart pads for the trainer and each team.

☐ Felt-tipped markers.

☐ Several rolls of masking tape.

☐ Name tents.

☐ Pens, pencils and writing pads for participants.

☐ Envelopes for Self Mail activity (p. 268).

Equipment

☐ Overhead projector.

☐ Flip chart stand for trainer and one for each team or table.

☐ Video-ready equipment.

Things to do

Prior to conducting the workshop, do the following:

 Prepare materials

Before you present the workshop, photocopy the workshop agenda and script. Write your planned start/stop times and anecdotal material on the photocopy.

Inquire about special needs

Meet with the director of training and several of the individuals enrolled in the course to learn about any special needs, internal issues, and the experience level of participants.

Develop relevant examples

Develop examples that are relevant to the industry or enterprise.

Encourage management participation

Invite a middle or top manager to kick off the workshop and emphasize the important role played by supervisors.

Facilities and Furniture

Room setup depends on the group's size and room's physical characteristics. Possible configurations are:

1. Team Tables

These coaching programs emphasize team participation—therefore, make sure the room setup provides sufficient tables and seating for each team.

2. Videotaping Exercises

For exercises which involve video replay, provide seats directly in front of the camera for those serving as behavior models, with enough seating in the back for the rest of the team.

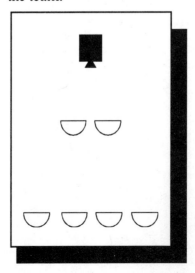

3. Breakout Rooms

Each breakout room should provide sufficient table seating for the team, with a flipchart within clear view of each participant.

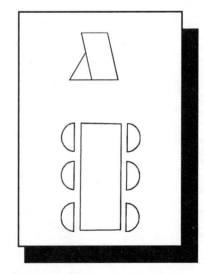

Audiovisual equipment

The facilitator's table, easels, and videocassette player should be positioned for clear viewing by all participants. The sound system should be adjusted so that everyone can hear videos, films, or words spoken into a microphone.

Power source

Find out where the climate control, light switches, electrical outlets, and sound system controls are. Also, obtain the name of the technician to call if you need assistance.

Supplies and refreshments

Place one table to the side for materials, supplies, and items such as a three-hole punch, stapler, and staple puller. If refreshments will be served, set those up on a second side table.

Facilities

Locate the phones, rest rooms, vending machines, and cafeteria so that you can direct participants to them. Get names of nearby lunch spots if lunch is not provided.

Name Tent

Superior Coaching Workshop

Participant Name

Superior Coaching Workshop

Participant Name

Participant Roster

Trainer(s): _____

Date: _____ **Time:** _____

Location: _____

_____

	Participant Name	Extension	Department
1.	_____	_____	_____
2.	_____	_____	_____
3.	_____	_____	_____
4.	_____	_____	_____
5.	_____	_____	_____
6.	_____	_____	_____
7.	_____	_____	_____
8.	_____	_____	_____
9.	_____	_____	_____
10.	_____	_____	_____
11.	_____	_____	_____
12.	_____	_____	_____
13.	_____	_____	_____
14.	_____	_____	_____
15.	_____	_____	_____
16.	_____	_____	_____
17.	_____	_____	_____
18.	_____	_____	_____
19.	_____	_____	_____
20.	_____	_____	_____

Workshop Certificate

Certificate of Achievement

This certifies that, on

_____
(date)

_____
(name)

successfully completed the

Superior Coaching Workshop

Congratulations!

_____
(Training Manager)

Chapter Four:

One-Hour Coaching Programs

This chapter contains two training plans for one-hour coaching programs—ready to go "as is" or to be tailored to meet your needs. The chapter is divided into four parts:

- Introduction.
- Materials Needed.
- Program Agenda.
- Two One-Hour Programs.

"THE SUPERIOR COACHING MODEL"

This program is designed to:

- Familiarize participants with the Superior Coaching Model.
- Ensure that participants understand each element in the model.
- Ensure that participants understand how the elements of the model are related to each other.

"CRITICAL SKILLS OF SUPERIOR COACHING"

This program is designed to:

- Reinforce participants' understanding of the Superior Coaching Model.
- Familiarize participants with the five critical skills of superior coaching.

Introduction

The one-hour coaching programs serve the following purposes:

- Provide an introduction to the subject of coaching.

- Reinforce some objectives or topics from previous programs.

- Present a series of related presentations about coaching, over a period of time, to extend previous learning.

There are numerous one-hour programs that trainers can give on coaching. It will be extremely difficult, however, to build coaching skills in one hour sessions—no matter how many of these you might conduct. Skill training requires:

- A clear understanding of the skill being learned.

- Time to practice the skill.

- Time to receive feedback on the performance of the skill.

- Time for more practice to benefit from the feedback.

One-Hour Topics

This section identifies topics for one-hour programs. If a topic has been covered previously, use the one-hour program to reinforce or expand upon a previous topic. If a topic has not been covered, use the one-hour program to introduce the topic. The point is, the topics may be the same; they are just being covered for different reasons. The topics are listed in two categories:

- Introductory topics.

- Reinforcement topics.

However, introductory topics can also be used to reinforce previous learning.

Introductory topics

Introductory topics used to acquaint participants with some aspect of superior coaching will usually be general and cover some sub-topic of the much larger topic of coaching. Programs to introduce coaching can be devoted to topics such as those found in Chapter 2:

- The definition and importance of coaching.

- The Superior Coaching Model.

- The key values of superior coaches.

- The essential characteristics of superior coaching.

- The critical skills of superior coaching.

- The core conversation of coaching.

- The performance applications of coaching.

Reinforcement topics

After a one-, two-, or three-day workshop, use one-hour sessions to reinforce certain aspects of the earlier training. All introductory topics listed above are also candidates for reinforcement sessions.

Once a larger topic has been introduced, such as the critical skills of superior coaching, use one-hour sessions to extend participants' learning about each of the critical skills:

- Attending.
- Inquiring.
- Reflecting.
- Affirming.
- Being disciplined.

Additional Topics

Listed below are additional topics for brief reinforcement sessions, or sessions to extend participants' learning.

If you use any of the interactive, videotaping and replay exercises, the time required will depend on the number of participants in each exercise group. You also must repeat these exercises so all participants have an opportunity to practice the skills. Topics to reinforce or extend previous learning are:

- Practicing being concrete.
- Practicing shared responsibility.
- Testing our understanding of creating shape.
- Practicing communicating respect.
- Practicing attending, inquiring, and reflecting.
- Practicing affirmation.
- Performance application: solving problems.
- Performance application: teaching.
- Performance application: supporting performance.
- Performance application: adjusting performance.

Customization Options

Almost any topic introduced in the one-, two-, and three-day work-shops can be turned into a module to fit a one-hour session. Train-ers may find it useful to reinforce previous learning by having participants repeat one of the Learning Activities in Chapter 9.

The following sections describe two examples of one-hour pro-grams. They can be used "as is" or as models for customized pro-grams, using any of the topics suggested above. We have assumed in these examples that the program is a true training program rather than merely a presentation. All topics can, of course, be adapted for use as presentations at conferences, conventions or other events attended by large groups. The two examples are:

- The Superior Coaching Model.
- The Critical Skills of Superior Coaching.

Materials Needed

These are the materials recommended for both one-hour coaching programs. Page references indicate where masters for the materials are found elsewhere in this book. Unless otherwise noted:

- For overhead transparencies, you will need one transparency each.

- For other items, you will need one per participant, plus a few spares.

The Superior Coaching Model

Overhead Transparencies

☐ Workshop Title and Trainer's Name (p. 289).

☐ Objectives for One-Hour Program:
The Superior Coaching Model (p. 291).

☐ The Superior Coaching Model (p. 306).

Handouts

☐ Understanding the Superior Coaching Model (p. 185).

☐ Workshop Evaluation—Short Form (p. 273).

Learning Activities

☐ Understanding the Superior Coaching Model (p. 185).

The Critical Skills of Superior Coaching

Overhead Transparencies

☐ Workshop Title and Trainer's Name (p. 289).

☐ Objectives for One-Hour Program:
The Critical Skills of Superior Coaching (p. 292).

☐ The Superior Coaching Model (p. 306).

☐ Critical Skills (p. 315).

Handouts

☐ Clarifying Critical Skills (p. 191).

☐ Workshop Evaluation—Short Form (p. 273).

Learning Activities

☐ Clarifying Critical Skills (p. 191).

Program Agenda

1. The Superior Coaching Model	Minutes 60	Start / Stop 8:00 / 9:00	Actual Start / Stop
Welcome and Administrative Details	5	8:00 / 8:05	_____ / _____
Program Overview	5	8:05 / 8:10	_____ / _____
Interactive Presentation: The Superior Coaching Model	10	8:10 / 8:20	_____ / _____
Understanding the Superior Coaching Model	20	8:20 / 8:40	_____ / _____
Debrief	5	8:40 / 8:45	_____ / _____
Program Review and Wrap-Up	10	8:45 / 8:55	_____ / _____
Evaluation	5	8:55 / 9:00	_____ / _____

2. The Critical Skills of Superior Coaching	Minutes 60	Start / Stop 8:00 / 9:00	Actual Start / Stop
Welcome and Administrative Details	5	8:00 / 8:05	_____ / _____
Program Overview	5	8:05 / 8:10	_____ / _____
Interactive Presentation: The Superior Coaching Model	10	8:10 / 8:20	_____ / _____
Clarifying Critical Skills	20	8:20 / 8:40	_____ / _____
Debrief	10	8:40 / 8:50	_____ / _____
Program Review and Wrap-Up	5	8:50 / 8:55	_____ / _____
Evaluation	5	8:55 / 9:00	_____ / _____

1. The Superior Coaching Model

FACILITATOR COMMENTARY

00:05   **Welcome and Administrative Details**

 WELCOME participants to this program on the Superior Coaching Model.

 SHOW the overhead, *Workshop Title and Trainer's Name* (p. 289).

 INTRODUCE yourself and give a brief summary of your qualifications and background.

REVIEW the following administrative details:

- Program length.
- Smoking policy.
- Location of rest rooms, telephones, and fire exits.

00:05   **Program Overview**

 SHOW the overhead, *Objectives for One-Hour Program: The Superior Coaching Model* (p. 291).

 MAKE the following points:

- Connect this program to any past coaching training that participants have had.
- Mention any future coaching training scheduled.

00:10   **Interactive Presentation: Superior Coaching Model**

 MAKE the following point:

- Emphasize that the model is results-oriented.

 SHOW the overhead, *The Superior Coaching Model* (p. 306).

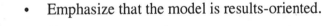 *DESCRIBE* briefly each element in the model:

- Key Values.
- Essential Characteristics.
- Critical Skills.
- Core Conversation.
- Performance Application.

ASK for and answer any questions participants have about the model and its elements.

GROUP ACTIVITY

00:20   **Understanding the Superior Coaching Model**

 DISTRIBUTE the handout, *Understanding the Superior Coaching Model* (p. 185).

REVIEW the exercise and its objectives. Assign breakout rooms, if used.

CALL time on the activity and return to the general session.

GROUP DISCUSSION

00:05   **Debrief**

 ASK for and answer any questions participants have about the model and its elements.

FACILITATOR COMMENTARY

00:10   **Program Review and Wrap-Up**

SHOW and *REVIEW* the overheads:

*   *Objectives for One-Hour Program* (p. 291).
*   *The Superior Coaching Model* (p. 306).

INDIVIDUAL ACTIVITY

00:05   **Evaluation**

DISTRIBUTE the *Workshop Evaluation—Short Form* (p. 273) to each participant.

Notes
*   _____
*   _____
*   _____
*   _____
*   _____
*   _____
*   _____
*   _____
*   _____
*   _____

2. The Critical Skills of Superior Coaching

FACILITATOR COMMENTARY

00:05 **Welcome and Administrative Details**

 WELCOME participants to this program on the critical skills of superior coaching.

 SHOW the overhead, *Workshop Title and Trainer's Name* (p. 289).

 INTRODUCE yourself and give a brief summary of your qualifications and background.

 REVIEW the following administrative details:

- Program length.
- Smoking policy.
- Location of rest rooms, telephones, and fire exits.

00:05 **Program Overview**

 SHOW the overhead, *Objectives for One-Hour Program: The Critical Skills of Superior Coaching* (p. 292).

 MAKE the following points:

- Connect this program to any past coaching training that participants have had.
- Mention any future coaching training scheduled.

00:10 **Interactive Presentation: Clarifying Critical Skills**

 SHOW the overhead, *The Superior Coaching Model* and describe its five elements (p. 306).

 SHOW the overhead, *Critical Skills* (p. 315).

 DESCRIBE each of the five critical skills:

- Attending.
- Inquiring.
- Reflecting.
- Affirming.
- Being Disciplined.

GROUP ACTIVITY

00:20   **Clarifying Critical Skills**

DISTRIBUTE the handout, *Clarifying Critical Skills* (p. 191).

REVIEW the exercise and its objectives. Assign breakout rooms, if used.

CALL time on the activity and return to the general session.

GROUP DISCUSSION

00:10   **Debrief**

ASK for and answer any questions participants have about the model and the critical skills.

FACILITATOR COMMENTARY

00:05   **Program Review and Wrap-up**

SHOW and *REVIEW* the overheads:

- *Objectives for the One-Hour Program* (p. 292).
- *The Superior Coaching Model* (p. 306).
- *Critical Skills* (p. 315).

INDIVIDUAL ACTIVITY

00:05   **Evaluation**

DISTRIBUTE the *Workshop Evaluation—Short Form* (p. 273) to each participant.

Notes

- _____
- _____
- _____
- _____
- _____
- _____
- _____
- _____
- _____

Chapter Five

Half-Day Coaching Program

This chapter contains training plans for a half-day coaching program—ready to go "as is" or to be tailored to meet your needs. The chapter is divided into five parts:

- Introduction.

- Half-Day Topics.

- Materials Needed.

- Program Agenda.

- Half-Day Program: Introduction to Superior Coaching.

"INTRODUCTION TO SUPERIOR COACHING"

This program is designed to:

- Help participants understand the importance of coaching as a leadership role.

- Introduce the Superior Coaching Model.

- Develop in participants a minimum understanding and skills to use the Superior Coaching Model.

Introduction

The half-day coaching programs can serve the same purposes as the one-hour designs. They can be used as:

- Introductions to the subject of coaching.

- Reinforcements on some objectives or topics of previous programs.

- A series of related programs presented over a period of time to extend previous learning.

Half-day programs obviously provide time to accomplish a lot more than one-hour sessions. In addition, the longer one-, two-, and three-day workshops can all be delivered in a spaced training format of two to six half-day sessions. Each of the longer programs can be separated at their mid-day points. The information about half-day programs that follows assumes that these:

- Are not half-day sessions of the one-, two-, or three-day programs.

- Will either introduce a coaching topic, reinforce previous learning, or extend previous learning.

As with the one-hour programs, there are numerous half-day programs trainers can give on coaching. The half-day programs differ from the one-hour programs in one important characteristic. Although it will be extremely difficult to build coaching skills in one-hour sessions, it is possible to do some skill training in the half-day sessions, especially if the sessions are used to reinforce or extend previous skills.

Half-Day Topics

This section identifies topics for half-day programs.

If a topic has been covered previously, use the half-day program to reinforce or expand upon a previous topic. If a topic has not been covered, use the half-day program to introduce the topic. As with one-hour programs, the topics may be the same; they are just being covered for different reasons.

The topics are listed in two categories:

- Introductory.

- Reinforcement.

However, introductory topics can also be used to reinforce previous learning.

Introductory topics

Introductory topics used to acquaint participants with some aspect of superior coaching will usually be general and cover some complete sub-topic of the much larger topic of coaching. Programs to introduce coaching can be devoted to topics such as those found in Chapter 2:

- The definition and importance of coaching.

- The Superior Coaching Model.

- The key values of superior coaches.

- The essential characteristics of superior coaching.

- The critical skills of superior coaching.

- The core conversation of superior coaching.

- The performance applications of superior coaching.

Reinforcement topics

Half-day programs used to reinforce previous learning or to build on some previous learning can be quite specific. After a one-, two-, or three-day workshop, use half-day sessions to reinforce certain aspects of the earlier training. All introductory topics listed above are also candidates for reinforcement sessions.

Once a larger topic has been introduced, such as the performance applications of superior coaching, use half-day sessions to practice each of the four applications:

- Resolving problems.

- Teaching.

- Supporting performance.

- Adjusting performance.

Additional Topics

Listed below are additional topics for reinforcement sessions, or sessions to extend participants' learning.

If you use any of the interactive, videotaping and replay exercises, the time required will depend on the number of participants in each exercise group. You also must repeat these exercises so all participants have an opportunity to practice the skills. Topics to reinforce or extend previous learning are:

- Understanding and using the essential characteristics.

- Understanding and using the critical skills.

- Performance application: solving problems.

- Performance application: teaching.

- Performance application: supporting performance.

- Performance application: adjusting performance.

Customization Options

Almost any topic introduced in the one-, two-, and three-day workshops can be turned into a module to fit a half-day session. Trainers may find it useful to reinforce previous learning by having participants repeat one of the Learning Activities in Chapter 9.

The following sections describe two examples of half-day programs. They can be used "as is" or as models for customized programs, using any of the topics suggested above. We have assumed in these examples that the program is a true training program rather than merely a presentation. All topics can, of course, be adapted for use as presentations at conferences, conventions or other events attended by large groups. The two examples are:

- The Superior Coaching Model.
- The Critical Skills of Superior Coaching.

Materials Needed

These are the materials recommended for the half-day coaching program. Page references indicate where masters for the materials are found elsewhere in this book. Unless otherwise noted:

- For overhead transparencies, you will need one transparency each.

- For other items, you will need one per participant, plus a few spares.

Overhead Transparencies

☐ Workshop Title and Trainer's Name (p. 289).

☐ Objectives for Half-Day Program: Introduction to Superior Coaching (p. 293).

☐ Half-Day Program Flow (p. 297).

☐ The Meaning of Superior Coaching (p. 305).

☐ The Superior Coaching Model (p. 306).

☐ Critical Skills (p. 315).

Handouts

☐ How the Jobs of Leading and Managing Are Changing and Why (p. 179).

☐ What Is Superior Coaching? (p. 183).

☐ Understanding the Superior Coaching Model (p. 185).

☐ Clarifying Critical Skills (p. 191).

☐ Workshop Evaluation—Short Form (p. 273).

Learning Activities

☐ Understanding the Superior Coaching Model (p. 185).

Program Agenda

Introduction to Superior Coaching	Minutes 3 hrs 10	Start / Stop 8:00 / 11:10	Actual Start/Stop
Welcome and Administrative Details	5	8:00 / 8:05	_____ / _____
Program Overview	5	8:05 / 8:10	_____ / _____
How the Jobs of Leading and Managing Are Changing and Why	25	8:10 / 8:35	_____ / _____
Debrief	10	8:35 / 8:45	_____ / _____
Interactive Presentation: The Definition of Superior Coaching	10	8:45 / 8:55	_____ / _____
What Is Superior Coaching?	25	8:55 / 9:20	_____ / _____
Debrief	10	9:20 / 9:30	_____ / _____
Break	15	9:30 / 9:45	_____ / _____
(Transition to next topic)	5	9:45 / 9:50	_____ / _____
Interactive Presentation: The Superior Coaching Model	10	9:50 / 10:00	_____ / _____
Understanding the Superior Coaching Model	20	10:00 / 10:20	_____ / _____
Debrief	5	10:20 / 10:25	_____ / _____
(Transition to next topic)	5	10:25 / 10:30	_____ / _____
Clarifying Critical Skills	25	10:30 / 10:55	_____ / _____
Debrief	5	10:55 / 11:00	_____ / _____
Program Review and Wrap-up	5	11:00 / 11:05	_____ / _____
Evaluation	5	11:05 / 11:10	_____ / _____

Introduction to Superior Coaching

FACILITATOR COMMENTARY

00:05　**Welcome and Administrative Details**

WELCOME participants to this program, Introduction to Superior Coaching.

SHOW the overhead, *Workshop Title and Trainer's Name* (p. 289).

INTRODUCE yourself and give a brief summary of your qualifications and background.

REVIEW the following administrative details:

- Program length.
- Smoking policy.
- Eating arrangements.
- How to get messages.
- Location of restrooms, telephones, and fire exits.

00:05　**Program Overview**

SHOW the overheads:

- *Objectives for Half-Day Program: Introduction to Superior Coaching* (p. 293).
- *Half-Day Program Flow* (p. 297).

MAKE the following points:

- Connect this program to any past coaching training that participants have had.
- Mention any future coaching training scheduled.

ASK for and answer any questions.

GROUP ACTIVITY

00:25

How the Jobs of Leading and Managing Are Changing and Why

DISTRIBUTE the handout, *How the Jobs of Leading and Managing Are Changing and Why* (p. 179).

REVIEW the exercise and its objectives. Assign breakout rooms, if used.

MAKE the following point:

- Participants should think concretely about their own experiences as leaders or observers of leaders in their own organizations.

CALL time on the activity and return to the general session.

GROUP DISCUSSION

00:10

Debrief

MAKE the following points:

- The control model of managing is disappearing.
- The coaching function is becoming a critical function of managers and leaders of companies due to:
  - downsizing.
  - reducing the direct supervision function.
  - using teams and teamwork as primary organizing principles.

ASK for and answer any questions.

INTERACTIVE PRESENTATION

00:10

Definition of Superior Coaching

MAKE the following point:

- Emphasize that superior coaching is results-oriented and disciplined.

Trainers should be very familiar with the section, The Definition of Superior Coaching, in Chapter 2.

SHOW the overhead, *The Meaning of Superior Coaching* (p. 305).

GROUP ACTIVITY

00:25   **What Is Superior Coaching?**

 DISTRIBUTE the handout, *What Is Superior Coaching?* (p. 183).

 REVIEW the exercise and its objectives. Assign breakout rooms, if used.

 MAKE the following point:

- Participants should think of their best coaches.

 CALL time on the activity and return to the general session.

GROUP DISCUSSION

00:10   **Debrief**

 MAKE the following point:

- Look for examples of what superior coaches do and how they do it.

00:15   **Break**

FACILITATOR COMMENTARY

00:05   **Transition to Superior Coaching Model**

 MAKE the following points:

- It is not just being a coach that is important, but being a *superior* coach.
- Superior coaches are disciplined.
- The model is a tool for developing discipline.

INTERACTIVE PRESENTATION

00:10   **Definition of Superior Coaching**

MAKE the following point:

- Emphasize that superior coaching is results-oriented.

SHOW the overhead, *The Superior Coaching Model* (p. 306) and leave up until transition.

DESCRIBE briefly each element in the model:

- Key Values.

- Essential Characteristics.

- Critical Skills.

- Core Conversation.

- Performance Applications.

GROUP ACTIVITY

00:20   **Understanding the Superior Coaching Model**

DISTRIBUTE the handout, *Understanding the Superior Coaching Model* (p. 185).

REVIEW the exercise and its objectives. Assign breakout rooms, if used.

MAKE the following point:

- Participants will be using the model in all future activities in the program.

CALL time on the activity and return to the general session.

GROUP DISCUSSION

00:05   **Debrief**

ASK for and answer any questions. Involve participants in answering the questions.

00:05   **Transition to Clarifying Critical Skills**

MAKE the following points:

- Participants will now look at individual elements in the model.

- Indicate which elements you will examine. (Time constraints require that not all elements can be examined.)

GROUP ACTIVITY

00:25   **Clarifying Critical Skills**

 SHOW the overhead, *Critical Skills* (p. 315) and leave up until review and wrap-up.

 DESCRIBE briefly each of the skills:

- Attending.

- Inquiring.

- Reflecting.

- Affirming.

- Being Disciplined.

 DISTRIBUTE the handout, *Clarifying Critical Skills* (p. 191).

 REVIEW the exercise and its objectives. Assign breakout rooms, if used.

 CALL time on the activity and return to the general session.

GROUP DISCUSSION

00:05   **Debrief**

 ASK for and answer any questions. Involve participants in answering the questions.

 MAKE the following points:

- Relate other elements in the Superior Coaching Model to critical skills.

- Superior coaching begins with what a person believes about how superior work is accomplished. From these values, a person creates the essential characteristics of superior coaching and then looks for the skills that create these characteristics.

FACILITATOR COMMENTARY

00:05   **Program Review and Wrap-Up**

     SHOW and *REVIEW* the overheads:

- *Objectives for the Half-Day Program* (p. 293).

- *The Superior Coaching Model* (p. 306).

- *Critical Skills* (p. 315).

INDIVIDUAL ACTIVITY

00:05   **Program Evaluation**

     DISTRIBUTE the *Workshop Evaluation—Short Form* (p. 273) to each participant.

     If this program is not a single event and is tied to prior or successive training, use the *Workshop Evaluation—Long Form.*

Notes
- _____
- _____
- _____
- _____
- _____
- _____
- _____
- _____
- _____
- _____
- _____
- _____
- _____
- _____
- _____
- _____
- _____
- _____

Chapter Six

One-Day Coaching Workshop

This chapter contains training plans for a one-day coaching workshop—ready to go "as is" or to be tailored to meet your needs. The chapter is divided into three parts:

- Materials Needed.

- Workshop Agenda.

- One-Day Workshop: The Importance of Coaching.

"THE IMPORTANCE OF COACHING"

This workshop is designed to:

- Help participants understand the importance of coaching as a leadership role.

- Introduce the Superior Coaching Model.

- Develop in participants a minimum understanding and skills to use the Superior Coaching Model.

Introduction

The one-day design is intended primarily as an introduction to coaching. Skill training and skill acquisition can only be minimally achieved. This design has particular value for introducing senior managers and other organizational leaders to coaching.

Also, if the two- or three-day programs are being used for different target groups, the one-day program can communicate to senior managers and other leaders the nature of these programs and sensitize them to their responsibilities to support such training.

Materials Needed

These are the materials recommended for the one-day coaching workshop. Page references indicate where masters for the materials are found elsewhere in this book. Unless otherwise noted:

- For overhead transparencies, you will need one transparency each.

- For other items, you will need one per participant, plus a few spares.

Overhead Transparencies

- ☐ The Superior Coaching Workshop (p. 289).

- ☐ Objectives for One-Day Workshop (p. 294).

- ☐ One-Day Program Flow (p. 298).

- ☐ Program Norms (p. 303).

- ☐ Why Coaching is Becoming So Important (p. 304).

- ☐ The Meaning of Superior Coaching (p. 305).

- ☐ Superior Coaching Model (p. 306).

- ☐ The Core Conversation (p. 307).

- ☐ The Four Performance Applications (p. 308).

- ☐ What Superior Coaches Believe (p. 309).

- ☐ Essential Characteristics (p. 311)

- ☐ The Meaning of Respect (p. 314).

- ☐ Critical Skills (p. 315).

Handouts

- ☐ Understanding the Superior Coaching Model (p. 185).

- ☐ Clarifying Key Values and Essential Characteristics (p. 187).

- ☐ Clarifying Critical Skills (p. 191).

- ☐ Clarifying the Core Conversation (p. 196).

- ☐ Clarifying Performance Applications (p. 198).

- ☐ What Superior Coaches Believe (p. 200).

- ☐ Practicing Communicating Respect (p. 217).

- ☐ Practicing Attending, Inquiring, and Reflecting (p. 225).

- ☐ Review and Action Logs, three per participant (p. 263).

- ☐ Workshop Evaluation—Long Form (p. 275-276).

Learning Activities (Trainer's Notes)

- ☐ Understanding the Superior Coaching Model (p. 184).

- ☐ Clarifying Key Values and Essential Characteristics (p. 186).

- ☐ Clarifying Critical Skills (p. 190).

- ☐ Clarifying the Core Conversation (p. 195).

- ☐ Clarifying Performance Applications (p. 197).

- ☐ What Superior Coaches Believe (p. 199).

- ☐ Practicing Communicating Respect (p. 216).

- ☐ Practicing Attending, Inquiring and Reflecting (p. 224).

Customization Options

To tailor the workshop to your particular group, do the following:

- For ease in distributing and referring to materials in class, create a numbered handout packet. Bind or staple the packet.

- Design a custom cover with the name of the sponsoring organization, date, and place of the workshop, and print it on heavy paper (cover stock).

- Distribute the packet when you begin the workshop and refer participants to appropriate pages throughout the day.

Workshop Agenda

1. The Importance of Coaching	Minutes 1 hr 40	Start / Stop 8:00 / 9:40	Actual Start / Stop
Welcome and Administrative Details	10	8:00 / 8:10	_____ / _____
Program Overview	10	8:10 / 8:20	_____ / _____
Program Norms	5	8:20 / 8:25	_____ / _____
Group Introductions	10	8:25 / 8:35	_____ / _____
Interactive Presentation: Why Coaching Is Becoming Such an Important Leadership Role	10	8:35 / 8:45	_____ / _____
Interactive Presentation: The Meaning of Superior Coaching	10	8:45 / 8:55	_____ / _____
(Transition to next topic)	5	8:55 / 9:00	_____ / _____
Interactive Presentation: The Superior Coaching Model	10	9:00 / 9:10	_____ / _____
Understanding the Superior Coaching Model	15	9:10 / 9:25	_____ / _____
Debrief	5	9:25 / 9:30	_____ / _____
Break	10	9:30 / 9:40	_____ / _____

2. Introducing the Superior Coaching Model	Minutes 2 hrs 40	Start / Stop 9:40 / 12:20	Actual Start / Stop
Transition to next topic	5	9:40 / 9:45	_____ / _____
Clarifying Key Values and Essential Characteristics	35	9:45 / 10:20	_____ / _____
Debrief	10	10:20 / 10:30	_____ / _____
Clarifying Critical Skills	25	10:30 / 10:55	_____ / _____
Debrief	10	10:55 / 11:05	_____ / _____
Clarifying the Core Conversation	15	11:05 / 11:20	_____ / _____
Debrief	5	11:20 / 11:25	_____ / _____
Review/Preview	10	11:25 / 11:35	_____ / _____
Lunch	45	11:35 / 12:20	_____ / _____

3. Performance Applications and Beliefs	Minutes 1 hr 20	Start / Stop 12:20 / 1:40	Actual Start / Stop
Clarifying Performance Applications	30	12:20 / 12:50	_____ / _____
Debrief	10	12:50 / 1:00	_____ / _____
(Transition to next topic)	5	1:00 / 1:05	_____ / _____
What Superior Coaches Believe	15	1:05 / 1:20	_____ / _____
Debrief	5	1:20 / 1:25	_____ / _____
(Transition to next topic)	5	1:25 / 1:30	_____ / _____
Break	10	1:30 / 1:40	_____ / _____

4. Skill Practice	Minutes 2 hrs 5	Start / Stop 1:40 / 3:45	Actual Start / Stop
Testing Our Understanding of Communicating Respect	30	1:40 / 2:10	_____ / _____
Debrief	10	2:10 / 2:20	_____ / _____
(Transition to next topic)	5	2:20 / 2:25	_____ / _____
Practicing Attending, Inquiring and Reflecting	45	2:25 / 3:10	_____ / _____
Debrief	10	3:10 / 3:20	_____ / _____
Review and Action Logs	10	3:20 / 3:30	_____ / _____
Workshop Review and Wrap-Up	10	3:30 / 3:40	_____ / _____
Evaluation	5	3:40 / 3:45	_____ / _____

The Importance of Coaching

Purpose   The one-day workshop is intended primarily as an introduction to coaching. Skill training and skill acquisition can only be minimally achieved. This design has particular value for introducing senior managers and other organizational leaders to coaching.

Objectives   The one-day workshop has been designed to help participants understand the importance of coaching as a leadership role, familiarize participants with the Superior Coaching Model, and provide participants with the minimum understanding and skills to use the Superior Coaching Model.

Workshop Agenda

1. The Importance of Coaching	Minutes 1 hr 40	Start / Stop 8:00 / 9:40	Actual Start / Stop
Welcome and Administrative Details	10	8:00 / 8:10	_____ / _____
Program Overview	10	8:10 / 8:20	_____ / _____
Program Norms	5	8:20 / 8:25	_____ / _____
Group Introductions	10	8:25 / 8:35	_____ / _____
Interactive Presentation: Why Coaching Is Becoming Such an Important Leadership Role	10	8:35 / 8:45	_____ / _____
Interactive Presentation: The Meaning of Superior Coaching	10	8:45 / 8:55	_____ / _____
(Transition to next topic)	5	8:55 / 9:00	_____ / _____
Interactive Presentation: The Superior Coaching Model	10	9:00 / 9:10	_____ / _____
Understanding the Superior Coaching Model	15	9:10 / 9:25	_____ / _____
Debrief	5	9:25 / 9:30	_____ / _____
Break	10	9:30 / 9:40	_____ / _____

Module 1   **The Importance of Coaching (8:00 to 9:40)**

FACILITATOR COMMENTARY

00:10   **Welcome and Administrative Details**

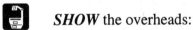 *WELCOME* participants to this workshop, The Superior Coaching Model.

SHOW the overhead, *Workshop Title and Trainer's Name*, (p. 289).

INTRODUCE yourself and give a brief summary of your qualifications and background.

REVIEW the following administrative details:

- Workshop length.
- Smoking policy.
- Breaks.
- Eating arrangements.
- How to get messages.
- Location of rest rooms, telephones, and fire exits.

00:10   **Workshop Overview**

SHOW the overheads:

- *Objectives for One-Day Workshop: The Superior Coaching Model* (p. 294).
- *One-Day Program Flow* (p. 298).

MAKE the following points:

- Connect this workshop to any past coaching training that participants have had.
- Mention any future coaching training scheduled.

00:05   **Program Norms**

 SHOW the overhead, *Program Norms* (p. 303).

 MAKE the following point:

- Norms set the way the program will be conducted and how participants are expected to perform.

ASK for and answer any questions.

GROUP ACTIVITY

00:10   **Group Introductions**

ASK participants to give their:

- Name.
- Job.
- Organization.
- Previous experience in coaching training programs.

This activity is only appropriate when the group is relatively small.

INTERACTIVE PRESENTATION

00:10   **Why Coaching Is an Important Leadership Role**

SHOW the overhead, *Why Coaching Is Becoming So Important* (p. 304).

MAKE the following points:

- The control model of managing is disappearing.
- Managers are more frequently becoming resources.
- Coaching is a primary tool for developing empowered people.

INTERACTIVE PRESENTATION

00:10   **The Meaning of Superior Coaching**

MAKE the following point:

- Emphasize that superior coaching is results-oriented and disciplined.

Trainers should be very familiar with the section, The Meaning of Superior Coaching, in Chapter 2.

SHOW the overhead, *The Meaning of Superior Coaching* (p. 305).

00:05   **Transition to Superior Coaching Model**

MAKE the following points:

- It is not just coaches that are important, but superior coaches.
- Superior coaches are disciplined.
- The model is a tool for developing discipline.

00:10   **Interactive Presentation: Superior Coaching Model**

 MAKE the following point:

- The model is results-oriented.

 SHOW the overhead, *The Superior Coaching Model* (p. 306).

 DESCRIBE briefly each element in the model:

- Key Values.
- Essential Characteristics.
- Critical Skills.
- Core Conversation.
- Performance Application.

 ASK for and answer any questions participants have about the model and its elements.

GROUP ACTIVITY

00:15   **Understanding the Superior Coaching Model**

 DISTRIBUTE the handout, *Understanding the Superior Coaching Model* (p. 185).

 REVIEW the exercise and its objectives. Assign breakout rooms, if used.

 MAKE the following point:

- Participants will be using the model in all future activities in the program.

 CALL time on the activity and return to the general session.

GROUP DISCUSSION

00:05   **Debrief**

 ASK for and answer any questions participants have about the model and its elements. Involve participants in answering the questions.

00:10   **Break**

Introducing the Superior Coaching Model

Purpose

This module of the one-day workshop provides an introduction to the Superior Coaching Model and its first three elements—key values, essential characteristics, and critical skills.

Participants are introduced to the concept of the core conversation and how it relates to the essential characteristics of the Superior Coaching Model.

Workshop Agenda

2. **Introducing the Superior Coaching Model**	**Minutes 2 hrs 40**	**Start / Stop 9:40 / 12:20**	**Actual Start / Stop**
(Transition to next topic)	5	9:40 / 9:45	_____ / _____
Clarifying Key Values and Essential Characteristics	35	9:45 / 10:20	_____ / _____
Debrief	10	10:20 / 10:30	_____ / _____
Clarifying Critical Skills	25	10:30 / 10:55	_____ / _____
Debrief	10	10:55 / 11:05	_____ / _____
Clarifying the Core Conversation	15	11:05 / 11:20	_____ / _____
Debrief	5	11:20 / 11:25	_____ / _____
Review/Preview	10	11:25 / 11:35	_____ / _____
Lunch	45	11:35 / 12:20	_____ / _____

| **Module 2** | **Introducing the Superior Coaching Model (9:40 to 12:20)** |

FACILITATOR COMMENTARY

00:05   **Transition to Clarifying Learning Activities**

 MAKE the following points:

- Participants will now look at individual elements in the model.
- Indicate which elements you will examine.

 Time constraints require that not all elements can be examined.

GROUP ACTIVITY

00:35   **Clarifying Key Values and Essential Characteristics**

 DISTRIBUTE the handout, *Clarifying Key Values and Essential Characteristics* (p. 187).

 REVIEW the exercise and its objectives. Assign breakout rooms, if used.

 CALL time on the activity and return to the general session.

GROUP DISCUSSION

00:10   **Debrief**

 ASK for and answer any questions.

 MAKE the following point:

- Ensure participants are beginning to see the Superior Coaching Model as a whole and how the individual elements are related to each other.

GROUP ACTIVITY

00:25   **Clarifying Critical Skills**

 DISTRIBUTE the handout, *Clarifying Critical Skills* (p. 191).

 SHOW the overhead, *Critical Skills* (p. 315).

DESCRIBE briefly each skill:

- Attending.
- Inquiring.
- Reflecting.
- Affirming.
- Being Disciplined.

REVIEW the exercise and its objectives. Assign breakout rooms, if used.

CALL time on the activity and return to the general session.

GROUP DISCUSSION

00:10   **Debrief**

ASK for and answer any questions.

GROUP ACTIVITY

00:15   **Clarifying the Core Conversation**

DISTRIBUTE the handout, *Clarifying the Core Conversation* (p. 196).

SHOW the overhead, *The Core Conversation* (p. 307).

MAKE the following point:
- It is important to understand the connection between:
    - Shape as a characteristic of the core conversation.
    - The way shape is developed during a superior coaching conversation.

REVIEW the exercise and its objectives. Assign breakout rooms, if used.

CALL time on the activity and return to the general session.

GROUP DISCUSSION

00:05   **Debrief**

ASK for and answer any questions.

MAKE the following points:

- The core conversation is the predictable shape that superior coaching conversations take.

- It is the process of moving from expanding information to focusing the use of this information that makes superior coaching so different from other kinds of coaching conversations.

SHOW the overheads, *The Superior Coaching Model* (p. 306) and *The Core Conversation* (p. 307).

FACILITATOR COMMENTARY

00:10   **Review/Preview**

SHOW the overhead, *Objectives for One-Day Workshop* (p. 294) and *REVIEW* those objectives.

SHOW the overhead, *The Meaning of Superior Coaching* (p. 305) and *REVIEW* the meaning.

SHOW the overhead, *Superior Coaching Model* (p. 306) and *REVIEW* the model.

MAKE the following points:

- The group has been clarifying its understanding of each element in the model.

- All elements have been covered, except the performance applications of coaching.

SHOW the overhead, *One-Day Program Flow* (p. 298).

MAKE the following comments:

After lunch we will:

- Examine the performance applications.

- Take a closer look at the elements of the model.

- Practice using the critical skills.

00:45   **Lunch**

Performance Applications and Beliefs

Purpose

This module of the one-day workshop helps participants clarify the final element in the Superior Coaching Model, performance applications.

Participants will learn about the beliefs of superior coaches and identify how these beliefs affect the behavior of superior coaches. Participants will then be given the opportunity to examine their own beliefs about coaching and compare these to the beliefs of superior coaches.

Workshop Agenda

3. Performance Applications and Beliefs	Minutes 1 hr 20	Start / Stop 12:20 / 1:40	Actual Start / Stop
Clarifying Performance Applications	30	12:20 / 12:50	_____ / _____
Debrief	10	12:50 / 1:00	_____ / _____
(Transition to next topic)	5	1:00 / 1:05	_____ / _____
What Superior Coaches Believe	15	1:05 / 1:20	_____ / _____
Debrief	5	1:20 / 1:25	_____ / _____
(Transition to next topic)	5	1:25 / 1:30	_____ / _____
Break	10	1:30 / 1:40	_____ / _____

Module 3   **Performance Applications and Beliefs (12:20 to 1:40)**

GROUP ACTIVITY

00:30   **Clarifying Performance Applications**

 DISTRIBUTE the handout, *Clarifying Performance Applications* (p. 198).

 SHOW the overhead, *The Four Performance Applications* (p. 308).

 REVIEW the exercise and its objectives. Assign breakout rooms, if used.

 CALL time on the activity and return to the general session.

GROUP DISCUSSION

00:10   **Debrief**

 ASK for and answer any questions.

 MAKE the following point:

- There are many different kinds of coaching conversations, but most pertain to one of the four types of performance applications:

  – Resolving Problems.

  – Teaching.

  – Supporting Performance.

  – Adjusting Performance.

 SHOW the overhead, *The Superior Coaching Model* (p. 306).

FACILITATOR COMMENTARY

00:05   **Transition to Key Values**

 MAKE this comment:

We have been gaining a general overview of the Superior Coaching Model and now will examine the elements in detail.

GROUP ACTIVITY

00:15   **What Superior Coaches Believe**

 DISTRIBUTE the handout, *What Superior Coaches Believe* (p. 200).

 SHOW the overhead, *What Superior Coaches Believe* (p. 309).

 REVIEW the exercise and its objectives. Assign breakout rooms, if used.

 CALL time on the activity and return to the general session.

GROUP DISCUSSION

00:05   **Debrief**

 ASK for and answer any questions.

 MAKE the following point:

- How beliefs influence one's views of coaching.

 Identify specific beliefs.

FACILITATOR COMMENTARY

00:05   **Transition to Essential Characteristics**

 MAKE the following comment:

We have looked at the first element in the Superior Coaching Model and are now looking at the second.

 SHOW the overheads, *The Superior Coaching Model* (p. 306) and *Essential Characteristics* (p. 311).

00:10   **Break**

Skill Practice

Purpose

This module of the one-day workshop gives participants the opportunity to practice the behaviors of attending, inquiring, and reflecting. Participants test their understanding of the meaning of respect and receive feedback concerning their performance.

Workshop Agenda

4. **Skill Practice**	Minutes 2 hrs 5	Start / Stop 1:40 / 3:45	Actual Start / Stop
Testing Our Understanding of Communicating Respect	30	1:40 / 2:10	_____ / _____
Debrief	10	2:10 / 2:20	_____ / _____
(Transition to next topic)	5	2:20 / 2:25	_____ / _____
Practicing Attending, Inquiring and Reflecting	45	2:25 / 3:10	_____ / _____
Debrief	10	3:10 / 3:20	_____ / _____
Review and Action Logs	10	3:20 / 3:30	_____ / _____
Workshop Review and Wrap-Up	10	3:30 / 3:40	_____ / _____
Evaluation	5	3:40 / 3:45	_____ / _____

Module 4   **Skill Practice (1:40 to 3:45)**

GROUP ACTIVITY

00:30   **Testing our Understanding of Communicating Respect**

 DISTRIBUTE the handout, *Practicing Communicating Respect* (p. 217).

 SHOW the overhead, *Meaning of Respect* (p. 314).

 REVIEW the exercise and its objectives. Assign breakout rooms, if used.

 CALL time on the activity and return to the general session.

GROUP DISCUSSION

00:10   **Debrief**

 ASK for and answer any questions.

 REVIEW the:
- List of essential characteristics:
  - Balance.
  - Being concrete.
  - Shared responsibility.
  - Shape.
  - Respect.
- Meaning of respect.

FACILITATOR COMMENTARY

00:05   **Transition to Critical Skills**

 SHOW the overhead, *The Superior Coaching Model* (p. 306).

 REVIEW the Superior Coaching Model and its elements.

 SHOW the overhead, *Critical Skills* (p. 315).

 MAKE the following comments:
- We have covered values and essential characteristics, and now turn to the third element, critical skills.
- Time does not permit looking at each skill in depth, so we will concentrate on the skills of attending, inquiring, and reflecting.

 Make certain that participants understand each of these skills. Give them concrete illustrations.

GROUP ACTIVITY

00:45   **Practicing Attending, Inquiring, and Reflecting**

 DISTRIBUTE the handout, *Practicing Attending, Inquiring, and Reflecting* (p. 225).

 REVIEW the exercise and its objectives. Assign breakout rooms, if used.

CALL time on the activity and return to the general session.

GROUP DISCUSSION

00:10   **Debrief**

 ASK for and answer any questions. Ask participants for examples of the three kinds of behavior practiced in the exercise.

GROUP ACTIVITY

00:10   **Review and Action Logs**

 DISTRIBUTE the *Review and Action Logs* (p. 263).

 ASK participants to complete a copy of the Review and Action log to record their key learnings.

 If time permits, have each team discuss the key learning points and jointly complete the logs.

MAKE the following point:

- The logs should be referred to after a few days to help remind participants of what they learned about superior coaching, and to encourage them to put their learning into practice.

FACILITATOR COMMENTARY

00:10   **Workshop Review and Wrap-Up**

 SHOW the overhead, *Objectives for One-Day Workshop* (p. 294) and *REVIEW* those objectives.

 SHOW the overhead, *The Meaning of Superior Coaching* (p. 305) and *REVIEW* the meaning.

 SHOW the overhead, *Superior Coaching Model* (p. 306) and *REVIEW* the model.

INDIVIDUAL ACTIVITY

00:05   **Workshop Evaluation**

DISTRIBUTE the *Workshop Evaluation—Long Form* to each participant (p. 275).

Notes

- _____
- _____
- _____
- _____
- _____
- _____
- _____
- _____
- _____
- _____
- _____
- _____
- _____
- _____
- _____
- _____
- _____
- _____
- _____
- _____
- _____

Chapter Seven:

Two-Day Coaching Workshop

This chapter contains training plans for a two-day coaching workshop—ready to go "as is" or to be tailored to meet your needs. The chapter is divided into four parts:

- Introduction.

- Materials Needed.

- Workshop Agenda.

- Two-Day Workshop.

"THE IMPORTANCE OF COACHING"

This workshop is designed to:

- Help participants understand the importance of coaching as a leadership role.

- Provide participants a clear understanding of the Superior Coaching Model.

- Equip participants with the minimum skills required to use the Superior Coaching Model.

- Give participants extensive feedback on how well they applied the Superior Coaching Model and skills in the two practice interactions.

- Provide participants an opportunity to plan how they will continue to reinforce their learning after the program, and how they will apply what they have learned to their jobs.

Introduction

The two-day workshop permits participants to do a great deal more than just learn about coaching and the Superior Coaching Model. They are involved in a number of skill building exercises, and on day two, they participate in two videotaped practice interactions in which they apply coaching skills to two of the four performance applications— teaching, resolving problems, supporting performance, and adjusting performance.

The two-day design provides a good foundation in coaching skills and participants can be offered additional training at some later date. Two practice interactions can be accomplished in the two-day design; follow-up programs can offer the other practice interactions.

Materials Needed

These are the materials recommended for the two-day coaching workshop. Page references indicate where masters for the materials are found elsewhere in this book. Unless otherwise noted:

- For overhead transparencies, you will need one transparency each.

- For other items, you will need one per participant, plus a few spares.

Overhead Transparencies

☐ Workshop Title and Trainer's Name (p. 289).

☐ Changes in Management and Leadership Functions (p. 290).

☐ Objectives for Two-Day Workshop (p. 295).

☐ Two-Day Program Flow (p. 299).

☐ The Meaning of Superior Coaching (p. 305).

☐ Superior Coaching Model (p. 306).

☐ The Core Conversation (p. 307).

☐ The Four Performance Applications (p. 308).

☐ What Superior Coaches Believe (p. 309).

☐ Essential Characteristics (p. 311).

☐ The Meaning of Respect (p. 314).

☐ Critical Skills (p. 315).

☐ Resolving Problems Performance Application (p. 316).

☐ Teaching Performance Application (p. 318).

☐ Supporting Performance Application (p. 320).

☐ Adjusting Performance Application (p. 322).

☐ Review and Action Teams (p. 324).

Handouts

☐ Why Coaching Is Becoming So Important (p. 181).

☐ Understanding the Superior Coaching Model (p. 185).

☐ Clarifying Key Values and Essential Characteristics (p. 187).

☐ Clarifying Critical Skills (p. 191).

☐ Clarifying the Core Conversation (p. 196).

☐ Clarifying Performance Applications (p. 198).

☐ What Superior Coaches Believe (p. 200).

☐ Practicing Communicating Respect (p. 217).

☐ Practicing Attending and Inquiring (p. 219).

☐ Practicing Attending, Inquiring and Reflecting (p. 225).

☐ Practice Interaction—Performance Application:
Resolving Problems (p. 232).

☐ Practice Interaction—Trainer's choice of Teaching, Supporting
Performance or Adjusting Performance (pp. 239-254).

☐ Review and Action Logs, three per participant (p. 263).

☐ Workshop Evaluation—Long Form (p. 275).

Learning Activities

☐ Why Coaching Is Becoming So Important (p. 180).

☐ Understanding the Superior Coaching Model (p. 184).

☐ Clarifying Key Values and Essential Characteristics (p. 186).

☐ Clarifying Critical Skills (p. 190).

☐ Clarifying the Core Conversation (p. 195).

☐ Clarifying Performance Applications (p. 197).

☐ What Superior Coaches Believe (p. 199).

☐ Practicing Communicating Respect (p. 216).

☐ Practicing Attending and Inquiring (p. 218).

☐ Practicing Attending, Inquiring, and Reflecting (p. 224).

☐ Practice Interaction—Performance Application: Resolving
Problems (p. 231).

☐ Practice Interaction—Trainer's choice of Teaching, Supporting
Performance, or Adjusting Performance (pp. 238-253).

Customization Options

To tailor the workshop to your particular group, do the following:

- For ease in distributing and referring to materials in class, create a numbered handout packet. Bind or staple the packet.

- Design a custom cover with the name of the sponsoring organization, date, and place of the workshop, and print it on heavy paper (cover stock).

- Distribute the packet when you begin the workshop and refer participants to appropriate pages throughout the day.

Workshop Agenda—Day One

1. The Importance of Coaching	Minutes 2 hrs 15	Start / Stop 8:00 / 10:15	Actual Start / Stop
Welcome and Administrative Details	10	8:00 / 8:10	_____ / _____
Program Overview	10	8:10 / 8:20	_____ / _____
Program Norms	5	8:20 / 8:25	_____ / _____
Group Introductions	10	8:25 / 8:35	_____ / _____
Organize Review and Action Teams and Introduce Review and Action Logs	15	8:35 / 8:50	_____ / _____
Why Coaching Is Becoming So Important	20	8:50 / 9:10	_____ / _____
Debrief	10	9:10 / 9:20	_____ / _____
Interactive Presentation: The Meaning of Superior Coaching	10	9:20 / 9:30	_____ / _____
(Transition to next topic)	5	9:30 / 9:35	_____ / _____
Interactive Presentation: The Superior Coaching Model	10	9:35 / 9:45	_____ / _____
Understanding the Superior Coaching Model	15	9:45 / 10:00	_____ / _____
Debrief	5	10:00 / 10:05	_____ / _____
Break	10	10:05 / 10:15	_____ / _____

2. Introducing the Superior Coaching Model	Minutes 2 hrs 20	Start / Stop 10:15 / 12:35	Actual Start / Stop
(Transition to next topic)	5	10:15 / 10:20	_____ / _____
Clarifying Key Values and Essential Characteristics	35	10:20 / 10:55	_____ / _____
Debrief	10	10:55 / 11:05	_____ / _____
Clarifying Critical Skills	25	11:05 / 11:30	_____ / _____
Debrief	10	11:30 / 11:40	_____ / _____
Review/Preview	10	11:40 / 11:50	_____ / _____
Lunch	45	11:50 / 12:35	_____ / _____

3. Performance Applications and Beliefs	Minutes 1 hr 35	Start / Stop 12:35 / 2:10	Actual Start / Stop
Clarifying the Core Conversation	15	12:35 / 12:50	_____ / _____
Debrief	5	12:50 / 12:55	_____ / _____
Clarifying Performance Applications	30	12:55 / 1:25	_____ / _____
Debrief	10	1:25 / 1:35	_____ / _____
(Transition to next topic)	5	1:35 / 1:40	_____ / _____
What Superior Coaches Believe	15	1:40 / 1:55	_____ / _____
Debrief	5	1:55 / 2:00	_____ / _____
Break	10	2:00 / 2:10	_____ / _____

4. Skill Practice	Minutes 1 hr 15	Start / Stop 2:10 / 3:25	Actual Start / Stop
(Transition to next topic)	5	2:10 / 2:15	_____ / _____
Practicing Communicating Respect	40	2:15 / 2:55	_____ / _____
Debrief	10	2:55 /3:05	_____ / _____
Review and Action Logs	10	3:05 / 3:15	_____ / _____
Review/Preview	10	3:15 / 3:25	_____ / _____

Workshop Agenda—Day Two

1. **Skill Practice**	**Minutes** **2 hrs 20**	**Start / Stop** **8:00 / 10:20**	**Actual** **Start / Stop**
Introduce Day Two	5	8:00 / 8:05	_____ / _____
Review and Action Logs	15	8:05 / 8:20	_____ / _____
(Transition to next topic)	5	8:20 / 8:25	_____ / _____
Practicing Attending and Inquiring	35	8:25 / 9:00	_____ / _____
Debrief	10	9:00 / 9:10	_____ / _____
Practicing Attending, Inquiring, and Reflecting	45	9:10 / 9:55	_____ / _____
Debrief	10	9:55 / 10:05	_____ / _____
(Transition to next topic)	5	10:05 / 10:10	_____ / _____
Break	10	10:10 / 10:20	_____ / _____

2. **Resolving Problems**	**Minutes** **2 hrs**	**Start / Stop** **10:20 / 12:20**	**Actual** **Start / Stop**
Interactive Presentation: Performance Application—Resolving Problems	15	10:20 / 10:35	_____ / _____
Performance Application—Resolving Problems	1:00	10:35 / 11:35	_____ / _____
Lunch	45	11:35 / 12:20	_____ / _____

3. Skill Practice	Minutes 4 hrs 30	Start / Stop 12:20 / 4:50	Actual Start / Stop
Performance Application—Resolving Problems (cont.)	1:00	12:20 / 1:20	_____ / _____
Debrief	10	1:20 / 1:30	_____ / _____
Interactive Presentation: Performance Application—Teaching, Supporting Performance, or Adjusting Performance (Trainer's choice)	15	1:30 / 1:45	_____ / _____
Break	10	1:45 / 1:55	_____ / _____
Performance Application—Trainer's choice selected in previous interactive presentation	2:00	1:55 / 3:55	_____ / _____
Debrief	10	3:55 / 4:05	_____ / _____
Review and Action Logs	20	4:05 / 4:25	_____ / _____
Workshop Review and Wrap-Up	10	4:25 / 4:35	_____ / _____
Evaluation	15	4:35 / 4:50	_____ / _____

The Importance of Coaching—Day One

Purpose

The first day of the two-day workshop gives participants the opportunity to explore the changing role of managing and leading and to become involved in a number of interactive skill building exercises.

Objectives

The two-day design provides a good foundation in coaching skills and participants can be offered additional training at some later date. Two practice interactions can be accomplished in the two-day design; follow-up programs can offer the other practice interactions.

Workshop Agenda

1. The Importance of Coaching	Minutes 2 hrs 15	Start / Stop 8:00 / 10:15	Actual Start / Stop
Welcome and Administrative Details	10	8:00 / 8:10	_____ / _____
Program Overview	10	8:10 / 8:20	_____ / _____
Program Norms	5	8:20 / 8:25	_____ / _____
Introductions	10	8:25 / 8:35	_____ / _____
Organize Review and Action Teams and Introduce Review and Action Logs	15	8:35 / 8:50	_____ / _____
Why Coaching Is Becoming So Important	20	8:50 / 9:10	_____ / _____
Debrief	10	9:10 / 9:20	_____ / _____
Interactive Presentation: The Meaning of Superior Coaching	10	9:20 / 9:30	_____ / _____
(Transition to next topic)	5	9:30 / 9:35	_____ / _____
Interactive Presentation: The Superior Coaching Model	10	9:35 / 9:45	_____ / _____
Understanding the Superior Coaching Model	15	9:45 / 10:00	_____ / _____
Debrief	5	10:00 / 10:05	_____ / _____
Break	10	10:05 / 10:15	_____ / _____

Module 1   **The Importance of Coaching (8:00 to 10:15)**

FACILITATOR COMMENTARY

00:10   **Welcome and Administrative Details**

 WELCOME participants to this workshop, The Importance of Coaching.

 SHOW the overhead, *Workshop Title and Trainer's Name* (p. 289).

 INTRODUCE yourself and give a brief summary of your qualifications and background.

 REVIEW the following administrative details:

- Workshop length.
- Smoking policy.
- Breaks.
- Eating arrangements.
- How to get messages.
- Location of rest rooms, telephones, and fire exits.

00:10   **Program Overview**

 SHOW the overheads, *Objectives for Two-Day Workshop: The Importance of Coaching* (p. 295) and *Two-Day Program Flow* (p. 299).

 MAKE the following points:

- Connect this workshop to any past coaching training that participants have had.
- Mention any future coaching training scheduled.

00:05   **Program Norms**

 SHOW the overhead, *Program Norms* (p. 303).

 MAKE the following point:

- Norms set the way the program will be conducted and how participants are expected to perform.

 ASK for and answer any questions.

GROUP ACTIVITY

00:10   **Group Introductions**

 ASK participants to give their:
- Name.
- Job.
- Organization.
- Previous experience in coaching training programs.

 This activity is only appropriate when the group is relatively small.

00:15   **Organize Review and Action Teams and Introduce Review and Action Logs**

 SHOW the overhead, *Review and Action Teams* (p. 324) and *EXPLAIN* the purpose of the teams.

 It is easiest to have participants seated initially with their Review and Action teams on the first day, even if you change seating on the following day.

DISTRIBUTE three copies of the *Review and Action Log* to each participant (p. 263).

MAKE the following points:
- Review and Action logs will be used throughout the workshop for participants to record what they have learned and how they might use what they have learned.
- Review and Action logs will be used in meetings of Review and Action teams to:
  - Identify key learning points.
  - Reinforce learning.
  - Identify opportunities to apply what has been learned.
- Teams should continue to meet after the workshop.

GROUP ACTIVITY

00:20   **Why Coaching Is Becoming So Important**

 SHOW the overhead, *Why Coaching Is Becoming So Important* (p. 304).

 DISTRIBUTE the handout, *Why Coaching Is Becoming So Important* (p. 181).

REVIEW the exercise and its objectives. Assign breakout rooms, if used.

Leave the definition of coaching open. Encourage participants to think about coaching in ways that are natural to them.

CALL time on the activity and return to the general session.

GROUP DISCUSSION

00:10   **Debrief**

ASK for and answer any questions.

SHOW the overhead, *Changes in Management and Leadership Functions* (p. 290).

Look for and emphasize ideas that suggest managers and leaders are doing:

- Less directing and controlling and more empowering of people.
- Less leading and managing by control and more managing and leading by commitment.

INTERACTIVE PRESENTATION

00:10   **The Meaning of Superior Coaching**

MAKE the following point:

- Superior coaching is results-oriented and disciplined.

Trainers should be very familiar with the section, The Meaning of Coaching, in Chapter 2.

SHOW the overhead, *The Meaning of Superior Coaching* (p. 305).

00:05   **Transition to Superior Coaching Model**

MAKE the following points:

- It is not just coaches who are important, but superior coaches.
- Superior coaches are disciplined.
- The model is a tool for developing discipline.

INTERACTIVE PRESENTATION

00:10   **Superior Coaching Model**

 MAKE the following point:

- Emphasize that the model is results-oriented.

 SHOW the overhead, *The Superior Coaching Model* (p. 306).

 DESCRIBE briefly each element in the model:

- Key Values.
- Essential Characteristics.
- Critical Skills.
- Core Conversation.
- Performance Application.

GROUP ACTIVITY

00:15   **Understanding the Superior Coaching Model**

 DISTRIBUTE the handout, *Understanding the Superior Coaching Model* (p. 185).

 REVIEW the exercise and its objectives. Assign breakout rooms, if used.

 MAKE the following point:

- Participants will be using the model in all future activities in the program.

⏳ *CALL* time on the activity and return to the general session.

GROUP DISCUSSION

00:05   **Debrief**

❓ *ASK* for and answer any questions participants have about the model and its elements. Involve participants in answering the questions.

00:10   **Break**

Introducing the Superior Coaching Model

Purpose   This module of the two-day workshop provides an introduction to
                       the Superior Coaching Model and its first three elements—
                       key values, essential characteristics, and critical skills.

                       Participants are introduced to the concept of the core conversation
                       and how it relates to the essential characteristics of the Superior
                       Coaching Model.

Workshop Agenda

2. **Introducing the Superior Coaching Model**	**Minutes 2 hrs 20**	**Start / Stop 10:15 / 12:35**	**Actual Start / Stop**
(Transition to next topic)	5	10:15 / 10:20	_____ / _____
Clarifying Key Values and Essential Characteristics	35	10:20 / 10:55	_____ / _____
Debrief	10	10:55 / 11:05	_____ / _____
Clarifying Critical Skills	25	11:05 / 11:30	_____ / _____
Debrief	10	11:30 / 11:40	_____ / _____
Review/Preview	10	11:40 / 11:50	_____ / _____
Lunch	45	11:50 / 12:35	_____ / _____

Module 2   **Introducing the Superior Coaching Model (10:15 to 12:35)**

FACILITATOR COMMENTARY

00:05   **Transition to Clarifying Learning Activities**

 MAKE the following points:
- Participants will now look at individual elements in the model.
- Indicate you will examine all elements, but emphasis will be placed on understanding and practicing the critical skills.

GROUP ACTIVITY

00:35   **Clarifying Key Values and Essential Characteristics**

 DISTRIBUTE the handout, *Clarifying Key Values and Essential Characteristics* (p. 187).

 REVIEW the exercise and its objectives. Assign breakout rooms, if used.

 CALL time on the activity and return to the general session.

GROUP DISCUSSION

00:10   **Debrief**

 ASK for and answer any questions.

 Ensure participants are beginning to see the Superior Coaching Model as a whole and how the individual elements are related to each other.

GROUP ACTIVITY

00:25   **Clarifying Critical Skills**

 DISTRIBUTE the handout, *Clarifying Critical Skills* (p. 191).

 SHOW the overhead, *Critical Skills* (p. 315).

 DESCRIBE briefly each skill:
- Attending.
- Inquiring.
- Reflecting.
- Affirming.
- Being disciplined.

REVIEW the exercise and its objectives. Assign breakout rooms, if used.

 CALL time on the activity and return to the general session.

GROUP DISCUSSION

00:10   **Debrief**

 ASK for and answer any questions.

FACILITATOR COMMENTARY

00:10   **Review/Preview**

 SHOW the overhead, *Objectives for Two-Day Workshop* (p. 295) and *REVIEW* those objectives.

 SHOW the overhead, *The Meaning of Superior Coaching* (p. 305) and *REVIEW* the meaning.

 SHOW the overhead, *Superior Coaching Model* (p. 306) and *REVIEW* the model.

 MAKE the following points:

- The group has been clarifying its understanding of each element in the model.

- All elements have been covered, except the performance applications of coaching.

 SHOW the overhead, *Two-Day Program Flow* (p. 299).

MAKE these comments:

After lunch we will:

- Examine the performance applications.

- Take a closer look at the elements of the model.

- Practice using the critical skills.

00:45   **Lunch**

Performance Applications and Beliefs

Purpose

This module of the two-day workshop helps participants clarify the final element in the Superior Coaching Model, performance applications.

Participants also learn about the beliefs of superior coaches and identify how these beliefs affect the behavior of superior coaches. Participants will then be given the opportunity to examine their own beliefs about coaching and compare these to the beliefs of superior coaches.

Workshop Agenda

3. Performance Applications and Beliefs	Minutes 1 hr 35	Start / Stop 12:35 / 2:10	Actual Start / Stop
Clarifying the Core Conversation	15	12:35 / 12:50	_____ / _____
Debrief	5	12:50 / 12:55	_____ / _____
Clarifying Performance Applications	30	12:55 / 1:25	_____ / _____
Debrief	10	1:25 / 1:35	_____ / _____
(Transition to next topic)	5	1:35 / 1:40	_____ / _____
What Superior Coaches Believe	15	1:40 / 1:55	_____ / _____
Debrief	5	1:55 / 2:00	_____ / _____
Break	10	2:00 / 2:10	_____ / _____

Module 3   **Performance Applications and Beliefs (12:35 to 2:10)**

GROUP ACTIVITY

00:15   **Clarifying the Core Conversation**

 DISTRIBUTE the handout, *Clarifying the Core Conversation* (p. 196).

 SHOW the overhead, *The Core Conversation* (p. 307).

 MAKE the following point:

It is important to understand the connection between:

- Shape as a characteristic of the core conversation.

- The way shape is developed during a superior coaching conversation.

 REVIEW the exercise and its objectives. Assign breakout rooms, if used.

 CALL time on the activity and return to the general session.

GROUP DISCUSSION

00:05   **Debrief**

 ASK for and answer any questions.

 MAKE the following points:

- The core conversation is the predictable shape that superior coaching conversations take.

- It is the process of moving from expanding information to focusing the use of this information that makes superior coaching so different from other kinds of coaching conversations.

 SHOW the overheads, *The Superior Coaching Model* (p. 306) and *The Core Conversation* (p. 307).

GROUP ACTIVITY

00:30   **Clarifying Performance Applications**

 DISTRIBUTE the handout, *Clarifying Performance Applications* (p. 198).

 SHOW the overhead, *The Four Performance Applications* (p. 308).

 REVIEW the exercise and its objectives. Assign breakout rooms, if used.

 CALL time on the activity and return to the general session.

GROUP DISCUSSION

00:10   **Debrief**

 ASK for and answer any questions.

 MAKE the following points:

There are many different kinds of coaching conversations, but most pertain to one of the four types of performance applications:

- Resolving Problems.
- Teaching.
- Supporting Performance.
- Adjusting Performance.

 SHOW the overhead, *The Superior Coaching Model* (p. 306).

FACILITATOR COMMENTARY

00:05   **Transition to Key Values**

 MAKE this comment:

We have been gaining a general overview of the Superior Coaching Model, and now will examine the elements in detail.

GROUP ACTIVITY

00:15   **What Superior Coaches Believe**

 DISTRIBUTE the handout, *What Superior Coaches Believe* (p. 200).

SHOW the overhead, *What Superior Coaches Believe* (p. 309).

REVIEW the exercise and its objectives. Assign breakout rooms, if used.

CALL time on the activity and return to the general session.

GROUP DISCUSSION

00:05   **Debrief**

ASK for and answer any questions.

MAKE the following points:

- How beliefs influence one's views of coaching.
- Identify specific beliefs.

00:10   **Break**

Notes

- _____
- _____
- _____
- _____
- _____
- _____
- _____
- _____
- _____
- _____
- _____
- _____
- _____
- _____
- _____
- _____
- _____

Skill Practice

Purpose   This module of the two-day workshop gives participants the opportunity to practice the behaviors of attending, inquiring, and reflecting. Participants test their understanding of the meaning of respect
and receive feedback concerning their performance.

Workshop Agenda

4. Skill Practice	Minutes 1hr 15	Start / Stop 2:10 / 3:25	Actual Start / Stop
(Transition to next topic)	5	2:10 / 2:15	_____ / _____
Practicing Communicating Respect	40	2:15 / 2:55	_____ / _____
Debrief	10	2:55 / 3:05	_____ / _____
Review and Action Logs	10	3:05 / 3:15	_____ / _____
Review/Preview	10	3:15/ 3:25	_____ / _____

Module 4   **Skill Practice (1:40 to 3:45)**

FACILITATOR COMMENTARY

00:05   **Transition to Essential Characteristics**

MAKE this comment:
We have looked at the first element in the Superior Coaching Model—key values—and are now looking at the second.

SHOW the overheads, *The Superior Coaching Model* (p. 306) and *Essential Characteristics* (p. 311).

GROUP ACTIVITY

00:40   **Practicing Communicating Respect**

DISTRIBUTE the handout, *Practicing Communicating Respect* (p. 217).

SHOW the overhead, *The Meaning of Respect* (p. 314).

REVIEW the exercise and its objectives. Assign breakout rooms, if used.

CALL time on the activity and return to the general session.

GROUP DISCUSSION

00:10   **Debrief**

ASK for and answer any questions.

ASK participants to give examples of statements that demonstrate respect and those that do not. Discuss how the statements differ.

MAKE this comment:
The goal is to develop a very concrete and behavioral understanding of respect.

GROUP ACTIVITY

00:10   **Review and Action Logs**

ASK participants to complete a copy of the Review and Action Log to record their key learnings.

If time permits, have each team discuss the key learning points and jointly complete the logs.

MAKE this comment:

The logs will be used with your Review and Action teams at the beginning of day two.

FACILITATOR COMMENTARY

00:10   **Review/Preview**

SHOW the overhead, *Objectives for Two-Day Workshop* (p. 295) and *REVIEW* the objectives.

SHOW the overheads, *Changes In Management And Leadership Functions* (p. 290) and *Why Coaching Is Becoming So Important* (p. 304).

REVIEW the key topics covered and the growing importance of coaching as a management and leadership function.

SHOW the overheads, *The Meaning of Superior Coaching* (p. 305) and *The Superior Coaching Model* (p. 306) and *REVIEW* their meaning.

SHOW the overhead, *Two-Day Program Flow* to *PREVIEW* day two.

Notes

- _____
- _____
- _____
- _____
- _____
- _____
- _____
- _____
- _____
- _____
- _____
- _____
- _____
- _____

The Importance of Coaching—Day Two

Purpose   This module of the two-day workshop gives participants the opportunity to practice the behaviors of attending, inquiring, and reflecting. Participants test their understanding of the meaning of respect and receive feedback concerning their performance.

Objectives   The two-day design provides a good foundation in coaching skills and participants can be offered additional training at some later date. Two practice interactions can be accomplished in the two-day design; follow-up programs can offer the other practice interactions.

Skill Practice

Purpose   This module provides reinforcement and skill practice for the key learning points from day one.

Participants engage in group activities to practice the critical skills *Attending*, *Inquiring*, and *Reflecting*.

Workshop Agenda

1. Skill Practice	Minutes 2 hrs 20	Start / Stop 8:00 / 10:20	Actual Start / Stop
Introduce Day Two	5	8:00 / 8:05	_____ / _____
Review and Action Logs	15	8:05 / 8:20	_____ / _____
(Transition to next topic)	5	8:20 / 8:25	_____ / _____
Practicing Attending and Inquiring	35	8:25 / 9:00	_____ / _____
Debrief	10	9:00 / 9:10	_____ / _____
Practicing Attending, Inquiring, and Reflecting	45	9:10 / 9:55	_____ / _____
Debrief	10	9:55 / 10:05	_____ / _____
(Transition to next topic)	5	10:05 / 10:10	_____ / _____
Break	10	10:10 / 10:20	_____ / _____

Module 1   **Skill Practice (8:00 to 10:20)**

FACILITATOR COMMENTARY

00:05   **Introduce Day Two**

 MAKE this comment:

Today you will meet in your Review and Action teams to review
key learning points from day one and discuss how you can apply
what you have learned. After this activity we will continue to
develop the Superior Coaching Model and look at the next element,
critical skills.

 ASK for and answer any questions.

GROUP ACTIVITY

00:15   **Review and Action Team Activity: Review and Action Logs**

 MAKE this comment:

The purpose of the Review and Action logs is to help you share and
reinforce your learning and to develop personal resources for continued learning and application.

 ASK the Review and Action teams to:

- Have each member share his/her Review and Action log.
- Clarify key learning points.
- Identify and discuss applications of what has been learned.

FACILITATOR COMMENTARY

00:05   **Transition to Critical Skills**

 SHOW the overheads, *The Superior Coaching Model* (p. 306) and
Critical Skills (p. 315).

 MAKE these comments:

- We have looked at the first two elements in the Superior
  Coaching Model—key values and essential characteristics—
  and are now looking at the third.
- Time does not permit looking at each skill in depth, so we will
  concentrate on the skills of attending, inquiring, and reflecting.

Make certain that participants understand each of these skills. Give
them concrete illustrations.

GROUP ACTIVITY

00:35   **Practicing Attending and Inquiring**

 DISTRIBUTE the handout, *Practicing Attending and Inquiring* (p. 219).

 SHOW the overhead, *Critical Skills* (p. 315).

 MAKE the following point:

- Emphasize the meaning of attending and inquiring.

 REVIEW the exercise and its objectives. Assign breakout rooms, if used.

 CALL time on the activity and return to the general session.

GROUP DISCUSSION

00:10   **Debrief**

 ASK for and answer any questions. Ask participants for examples of attending and inquiring.

GROUP ACTIVITY

00:45   **Practicing Attending, Inquiring and Reflecting**

 DISTRIBUTE the handout, *Practicing Attending, Inquiring, and Reflecting* (p. 225).

 SHOW the overhead, *Critical Skills* (p. 315).

 REVIEW the exercise and its objectives. Assign breakout rooms, if used.

CALL time on the activity and return to the general session.

GROUP DISCUSSION

00:10   **Debrief**

ASK for and answer any questions. Ask for examples from participants of the three kinds of behavior practiced in the exercise.

FACILITATOR COMMENTARY

00:05   **Transition to Performance Applications**

SHOW the overheads, *The Superior Coaching Model* (p. 306) and *The Four Performance Applications* (p. 308).

MAKE the following points:

- Review the Superior Coaching Model and its elements.

- Emphasize that everything in the model leads to the performance applications, which can make a difference in the performance of individuals and teams.

00:10   **Break**

Notes

- _____

- _____

- _____

- _____

- _____

- _____

- _____

- _____

- _____

- _____

- _____

- _____

- _____

- _____

- _____

- _____

- _____

- _____

Resolving Problems

Purpose

This module of the two-day workshop gives participants the opportunity to practice all the elements in the Superior Coaching Model and apply the elements to a performance application that focuses on resolving problems. Participants are given feedback on their demonstrated competency in using the Superior Coaching Model and using it in the performance application, *Resolving Problems*.

Workshop Agenda

2. Resolving Problems	Minutes 2 hrs	Start / Stop 10:20 / 12:20	Actual Start / Stop
Interactive Presentation— Performance Application: Resolving Problems	15	10:20 / 10:35	_____ / _____
Performance Application: Resolving Problems	1:00	10:35 / 11:35	_____ / _____
Lunch	45	11:35 / 12:20	_____ / _____

Module 2   **Resolving Problems (10:20 to 12:20)**

INTERACTIVE PRESENTATION

00:15   **Performance Application: Resolving Problems**

SHOW the overhead, *Resolving Problems Performance Application* (p. 316).

DESCRIBE the special characteristics of the resolving problems application. Identify what the coach is accomplishing in the expanding and focusing phases of the conversation.

PRACTICE INTERACTION

01:00   **Performance Application: Resolving Problems**

DISTRIBUTE the handout, *Practice Interaction—Performance Application: Resolving Problems* (p. 232).

SHOW the overhead, *The Four Performance Applications* (p. 308) and *REVIEW* the applications.

SHOW the overhead, *Resolving Problems Performance Applications* (p. 316) and *REVIEW* the Resolving Problems performance application.

Ensure that the meaning of resolving problems is clear. Advise participants to return to the exercise directly after lunch.

_____

00:45   **Lunch**

_____

Notes   • _____

               • _____

               • _____

               • _____

               • _____

               • _____

               • _____

               • _____

               • _____

Skill Practice

Purpose

This module of the two-day workshop provides reinforcement and skill practice for the performance application, *Resolving Problems.*

Participants engage in an interactive presentation and practice interaction based on the performance application of the trainer's choice: *Teaching*, *Supporting Performance*, or *Adjusting Performance.*

Workshop Agenda

3. Skill Practice	Minutes 4 hrs 30	Start / Stop 12:20 / 4:50	Actual Start / Stop
Performance Application: Resolving Problems (cont.)	1:00	12:20 / 1:20	_____ / _____
Debrief	10	1:20 / 1:30	_____ / _____
Interactive Presentation—Performance Application: Teaching, Supporting Performance, or Adjusting Performance (Trainer's choice)	15	1:30 / 1:45	_____ / _____
Break	10	1:45 / 1:55	_____ / _____
Practice Interaction: Trainer's choice selected in previous interactive presentation	2:00	1:55 / 3:55	_____ / _____
Debrief	10	3:55 / 4:05	_____ / _____
Review and Action Logs	20	4:05 / 4:25	_____ / _____
Workshop Review and Wrap-Up	10	4:25 / 4:35	_____ / _____
Evaluation	15	4:35 / 4:50	_____ / _____

Module 3   **Skill Practice (12:20 to 4:50)**

PRACTICE INTERACTION (CONT.)

01:00   **Performance Application: Resolving Problems**

CALL time on the activity and return to the general session.

GROUP DISCUSSION

00:10   **Debrief**

ASK for and answer any questions and discuss the participants' key learnings.

INTERACTIVE PRESENTATION

00:15   **Trainer's Choice:**
                   Supporting Performance or Adjusting Performance

SHOW the appropriate overhead:
- *Teaching Performance Application* (p. 318).
- *Supporting Performance Application* (p. 320).
- *Adjusting Performance Application* (p. 322).

DESCRIBE the special characteristics of the application you selected. Identify what the coach is accomplishing in the expanding and focusing phases of the conversation.

00:10   **Break**

02:00   **Trainer's Choice: Performance Application**

DISTRIBUTE the appropriate handout:
- *Teaching* (p. 239).
- *Supporting Performance* (p. 245).
- *Adjusting Performance* (p. 254).

SHOW the appropriate overhead:

- *Teaching Performance Application* (p. 318).
- *Supporting Performance Application* (p. 320).
- *Adjusting Performance Application* (p. 322).

REVIEW the application and ensure that its meaning is clear.

CALL time on the activity and return to the general session.

GROUP DISCUSSION

00:10   **Debrief**

ASK for and answer any questions and discuss the participants' key learnings.

REVIEW AND ACTION TEAM

00:20   **Review and Action Logs**

ASK the Review and Action teams to:

- Review their key learnings.

- Refer to their first Review and Action log that they completed at the end of day one.

- Complete their logs for day two.

- Discuss their logs.

MAKE the following point if participants are from the same organization:

Encourage them to commit to a follow-up meeting at a later date to reinforce their learning and support each other's work at becoming superior coaches.

FACILITATOR COMMENTARY

00:10   **Workshop Review and Wrap-Up**

SHOW the overhead, *Objectives for Two-Day Workshop* (p. 295) and *REVIEW* the objectives.

SHOW the overheads, *Changes in Management and Leadership Functions* (p. 290), *Why Coaching Is Becoming So Important* (p. 304), and *Two-Day Program Flow* (p. 299).

REVIEW the key topics covered:

- The growing importance of coaching as a management and leadership function.

- The critical skills and performance applications.

SHOW the overheads, *The Meaning of Superior Coaching* (p. 305) and *The Superior Coaching Model* (p. 306).

REVIEW the model and its elements.

INDIVIDUAL ACTIVITY

00:15   **Evaluation**

DISTRIBUTE the *Workshop Evaluation—Long Form* to each participant (p. 275).

Notes

- _____
- _____
- _____
- _____
- _____
- _____
- _____
- _____
- _____
- _____
- _____
- _____
- _____
- _____
- _____
- _____
- _____
- _____

Chapter Eight

Three-Day Coaching Workshop

This chapter contains training plans for a three-day coaching workshop—ready to go "as is" or to be tailored to meet your needs. The chapter is divided into four parts:

- Introduction.
- Workshop Agenda.
- Materials Needed.
- Three-Day Workshop.

"THE IMPORTANCE OF COACHING"

This workshop is designed to:

- Help participants understand the importance of coaching as a leadership role.
- Provide participants a clear understanding of the Superior Coaching Model.
- Provide participants with an in-depth understanding of each element in the model and how all elements are related to each other.
- Equip participants with all skills required to use the Superior Coaching Model.
- Give participants extensive feedback on how well they applied the Superior Coaching Model and skills in the two practice interactions.
- Provide participants an opportunity to plan how they will continue to reinforce their learning after the program, and how they will apply what they have learned to their jobs.

Introduction

The three-day coaching workshop is preferred over other designs because it is most complete. It provides the best opportunity for a full understanding of the Superior Coaching Model and how to translate the model into behavior on the job, and, through the use of Review and Action teams, it provides the most assurance that what is learned in the training program will improve individual and organizational performance.

Materials Needed

These are the materials recommended for the three-day coaching workshop. Page references indicate where masters for the materials are found elsewhere in this book. Unless otherwise noted:

- For overhead transparencies, you will need one transparency each.

- For other items, you will need one per participant, plus a few spares.

Overhead Transparencies

☐ Workshop Title and Trainer's Name (p. 289).

☐ Changes in Management and Leadership Functions (p. 290).

☐ Objectives for Three-Day Workshop (p. 296).

☐ Three-Day Program Flow (p. 301).

☐ Meaning of Superior Coaching (p. 305).

☐ The Superior Coaching Model (p. 306).

☐ The Core Conversation (p. 307).

☐ The Four Performance Applications (p. 308).

☐ What Superior Coaches Believe (p. 309).

☐ Essential Characteristics (p. 311).

☐ The Meaning of Balance (p. 312).

☐ The Meaning of Being Concrete (p. 313).

☐ Critical Skills (p. 315).

☐ Resolving Problems Performance Application (p. 316).

☐ Teaching Performance Application (p. 318).

☐ Supporting Performance Application (p. 320).

☐ Adjusting Performance Application (p. 322).

☐ Review and Action Teams (p. 324).

Handouts

☐ Why Coaching Is Becoming So Important (p. 181).

☐ What Is Superior Coaching? (p. 183).

☐ Understanding the Superior Coaching Model (p. 185).

☐ Clarifying Key Values and Essential Characteristics (p. 187).

☐ Clarifying Critical Skills (p. 191).

☐ Clarifying the Core Conversation (p. 196).

☐ Clarifying Performance Applications (p. 198).

☐ What Superior Coaches Believe (p. 200).

☐ Testing Our Understanding of Creating Balance (p. 202).

☐ Practicing Being Concrete (p. 204).

☐ Practicing Developing Shared Responsibility (p. 206).

☐ Testing Our Understanding of Creating Shape (p. 209).

☐ Practicing Communicating Respect (p. 217).

☐ Practicing Attending and Inquiring (p. 219).

☐ Practicing Reflecting (p. 222).

☐ Practicing Affirming (p. 228).

☐ Practice Interaction—Performance Application: Resolving Problems (p. 232).

☐ Practice Interaction—Teaching, Supporting Performance, or Adjusting Performance (Trainer's choice) (pp. 239-254).

☐ Review and Action Logs (p. 263).

☐ Workshop Evaluation—Long Form (p. 275).

Learning Activities (Trainer's Notes)

☐ Why Coaching Is Becoming So Important (p. 180).

☐ What Is Superior Coaching? (p. 182).

☐ Understanding the Superior Coaching Model (p. 184).

☐ Clarifying Key Values and Essential Characteristics (p. 186).

☐ Clarifying Critical Skills (p. 190).

☐ Clarifying the Core Conversation (p. 195).

☐ Clarifying Performance Applications (p. 197).

☐ What Superior Coaches Believe (p. 199).

☐ Testing Our Understanding of Creating Balance (p. 201).

☐ Practicing Being Concrete (p. 203).

☐ Practicing Developing Shared Responsibility (p. 205).

☐ Testing Our Understanding of Creating Shape (p. 208).

☐ Practicing Communicating Respect (p. 216).

☐ Practicing Attending and Inquiring (p. 218).

☐ Practicing Reflecting (p. 221).

☐ Practicing Affirming (p. 227).

☐ Practice Interaction—Performance Application: Resolving Problems (p. 231).

☐ Practice Interaction—Teaching, Supporting Performance, or Adjusting Performance (Trainer's choice) (pp. 238-252).

Customization Options

To tailor the workshop to your particular group, do the following:

- For ease in distributing and referring to materials in class, create a numbered handout packet. Bind or staple the packet.

- Design a custom cover with the name of the sponsoring organization, date, and place of the workshop, and print it on heavy paper (cover stock).

- Distribute the packet when you begin the workshop and refer participants to appropriate pages throughout the day.

Workshop Agenda—Day One

1. The Importance of Coaching	Minutes 2 hrs	Start / Stop 8:00 / 10:00	Actual Start / Stop
Welcome and Administrative Details	10	8:00 / 8:10	_____ / _____
Workshop Overview	10	8:10 / 8:20	_____ / _____
Workshop Norms	5	8:20 / 8:25	_____ / _____
Introductions	10	8:25 / 8:35	_____ / _____
Organize Review and Action Teams and Introduce Review and Action Logs	15	8:35 / 8:50	_____ / _____
Why Coaching Is Becoming So Important	20	8:50 / 9:10	_____ / _____
Debrief	10	9:10 / 9:20	_____ / _____
What Is Superior Coaching?	20	9:20 / 9:40	_____ / _____
Debrief	10	9:40 / 9:50	_____ / _____
Break	10	9:50 / 10:00	_____ / _____

2. The Superior Coaching Model (Part I)	Minutes 2 hrs 30	Start / Stop 10:00 / 12:30	Actual Start / Stop
Interactive Presentation: The Meaning of Superior Coaching	10	10:00 / 10:10	_____ / _____
(Transition to next topic)	5	10:10 / 10:15	_____ / _____
Interactive Presentation: The Superior Coaching Model	10	10:15 / 10:25	_____ / _____
Understanding the Superior Coaching Model	15	10:25 / 10:40	_____ / _____
Debrief	5	10:40 / 10:45	_____ / _____
(Transition to next topic)	5	10:45 / 10:50	_____ / _____
Clarifying Key Values and Essential Characteristics	35	10:50 / 11:25	_____ / _____
Debrief	10	11:25 / 11:35	_____ / _____
Review/Preview	10	11:35 / 11:45	_____ / _____
Lunch	45	11:45 / 12:30	_____ / _____

3. The Superior Coaching Model (Part II)	**Minutes 1 hr 45**	**Start / Stop 12:30 / 2:15**	**Actual Start / Stop**
Clarifying Critical Skills	25	12:30 / 12:55	_____ / _____
Debrief	10	12:55 / 1:05	_____ / _____
Clarifying the Core Conversation	15	1:05 / 1:20	_____ / _____
Debrief	5	1:20 / 1:25	_____ / _____
Clarifying Performance Applications	30	1:25 / 1:55	_____ / _____
Debrief	10	1:55 / 2:05	_____ / _____
Break	10	2:05/ 2:15	_____ / _____

4 · Values and Beliefs	**Minutes 1 hr 20**	**Start / Stop 2:15 / 3:35**	**Actual Start / Stop**
(Transition to next topic)	5	2:15 / 2:20	_____ / _____
What Superior Coaches Believe	35	2:20 / 2:55	_____ / _____
Debrief	10	2:55 / 3:05	_____ / _____
Review and Action Teams Activity	20	3:05 / 3:25	_____ / _____
Review/Preview	10	3:25 / 3:35	_____ / _____

Workshop Agenda—Day Two

1. Essential Characteristics (Part I)	Minutes 2 hrs 35	Start / Stop 8:00 / 10:35	Actual Start / Stop
Introduce Day Two	15	8:00 / 8:15	_____ / _____
(Transition to next topic)	5	8:15 / 8:20	_____ / _____
Testing Our Understanding of Creating Balance	30	8:20 / 8:50	_____ / _____
Debrief	10	8:50 / 9:00	_____ / _____
Practicing Being Concrete	35	9:00 / 9:35	_____ / _____
Debrief	10	9:35 / 9:45	_____ / _____
Practicing Developing Shared Responsibility	35	9:45 / 10:20	_____ / _____
Debrief	5	10:20 / 10:25	_____ / _____
Break	10	10:25 / 10:35	_____ / _____

2. Essential Characteristics (Part II)	Minutes 2 hrs 15	Start / Stop 10:35 / 12:50	Actual Start / Stop
Testing Our Understanding of Shape (The Core Conversation)	30	10:35 / 11:05	_____ / _____
Debrief	10	11:05 / 11:15	_____ / _____
Testing Our Understanding of Communicating Respect	30	11:15 / 11:45	_____ / _____
Debrief	10	11:45 / 11:55	_____ / _____
Review/Preview	10	11:55 / 12:05	_____ / _____
Lunch	45	12:05 / 12:50	_____ / _____

3. Critical Skills	Minutes 2 hrs 50	Start / Stop 12:50 / 3:40	Actual Start / Stop
(Transition to next topic)	5	12:50 / 12:55	_____ / _____
Practicing Attending and Inquiring	35	12:55 / 1:30	_____ / _____
Debrief	10	1:30 / 1:40	_____ / _____
Practicing Reflecting	35	1:40 / 2:15	_____ / _____
Break	10	2:15 / 2:25	
Debrief	10	2:25 / 2:35	_____ / _____
Practicing Affirming	30	2:35 / 3:05	_____ / _____
Debrief	5	3:05 / 3:10	_____ / _____
Review and Action Logs	20	3:10 / 3:30	_____ / _____
Review/Preview	10	3:30 / 3:40	_____ / _____

Workshop Agenda—Day Three

1. Resolving Problems	Minutes 3 hrs 45	Start / Stop 8:00 / 11:45	Actual Start / Stop
Introduce Day Three	15	8:00 / 8:15	_____ / _____
Review Meaning of Superior Coaching and the Superior Coaching Model	15	8:15 / 8:30	_____ / _____
(Transition to next topic)	5	8:30 / 8:35	_____ / _____
Interactive Presentation—Performance Application: Resolving Problems	15	8:35 / 8:50	_____ / _____
Performance Application: Resolving Problems	2:00	8:50 / 10:50	_____ / _____
Debrief	10	10:50 / 11:00	_____ / _____
Lunch	45	11:00 / 11:45	_____ / _____

2. Skill Practice	Minutes 3 hrs 40	Start / Stop 11:45 / 3:25	Actual Start / Stop
Review and Action Teams Activity	30	11:45 / 12:15	_____ / _____
Interactive Presentation—Performance Application: Teaching, Supporting Performance, Adjusting Performance (Trainer's choice)	15	12:15 / 12:30	_____ / _____
Performance Application: Selected in previous interactive presentation (Trainer's choice)	2:00	12:30 / 2:30	_____ / _____
Debrief	10	2:30 / 2:40	_____ / _____
Review and Action Logs	20	2:40 / 3:00	_____ / _____
Workshop Review and Wrap-up	10	3:00 / 3:10	_____ / _____
Evaluation	15	3:10 / 3:25	_____ / _____

Importance of Coaching—Day One

Purpose   The first day of the three-day workshop gives participants the opportunity to explore the changing role of managing and leading and to become involved in a number of interactive skill building exercises.

Objectives   The three-day design provides the best opportunity to develop a good foundation in coaching skills, and, through the use of Review and Action teams, provides the most assurance that what is learned in the training program will improve individual and organizational performance.

Workshop Agenda

1. The Importance of Coaching	Minutes 2 hrs	Start / Stop 8:00 / 10:00	Actual Start / Stop
Welcome and Administrative Details	10	8:00 / 8:10	_____ / _____
Workshop Overview	10	8:10 / 8:20	_____ / _____
Workshop Norms	5	8:20 / 8:25	_____ / _____
Introductions	10	8:25 / 8:35	_____ / _____
Organize R&A Teams and Introduce Review and Action Logs	15	8:35 / 8:50	_____ / _____
Why Coaching Is Becoming So Important	20	8:50 / 9:10	_____ / _____
Debrief	10	9:10 / 9:20	_____ / _____
What Is Superior Coaching?	20	9:20 / 9:40	_____ / _____
Debrief	10	9:40 / 9:50	_____ / _____
Break	10	9:50 / 10:00	_____ / _____

Module 1   **The Importance of Coaching (8:00 to 10:00)**

FACILITATOR COMMENTARY

00:10   **Welcome and Administrative Details**

WELCOME participants to this workshop, The Importance of Coaching.

SHOW the overhead, *Workshop Title and Trainer's Name* (p. 289).

INTRODUCE yourself and give a brief summary of your qualifications and background.

REVIEW the following administrative details:

- Charge numbers.
- Workshop length.
- Smoking policy.
- Breaks.
- Eating arrangements.
- How to get messages.
- Location of restrooms, telephones, and fire exits.

00:10   **Workshop Overview**

SHOW the overheads *Objectives for Three-Day Workshop: The Importance of Coaching* (p. 296) and *Three-Day Program Flow* (p. 301).

MAKE the following points:

- Connect this workshop to any past coaching training that participants have had.
- Mention any future coaching training scheduled.

00:05   **Program Norms**

SHOW the overhead, *Program Norms* (p. 303).

MAKE the following point:

- Norms set the way the program will be conducted and how participants are expected to perform.

ASK for and answer any questions.

GROUP ACTIVITY

00:10   **Group Introductions**

 ASK participants to give their:

- Name.

- Job.

- Organization.

- Previous experience in coaching training programs.

 This activity is only appropriate when the group is relatively small.

00:15   **Organize Review and Action Teams and Introduce Review and Action Logs**

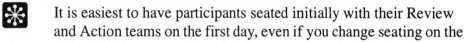 *SHOW* the overhead, *Review and Action Teams* (p. 324) and *EXPLAIN* the purpose of the teams.

 It is easiest to have participants seated initially with their Review and Action teams on the first day, even if you change seating on the following day.

DISTRIBUTE three copies of the *Review and Action Log* to each participant (p. 263).

MAKE the following points:

- Review and Action logs will be used throughout the workshop for participants to record what they have learned and how they might use what they have learned.

- Review and Action logs will be used in meetings of Review and Action teams to:

  – Identify key learning points.

  – Reinforce learning.

  – Identify opportunities to apply what has been learned.

- Teams should continue to meet after the workshop.

GROUP ACTIVITY

00:20   **Why Coaching Is Becoming So Important**

SHOW the overhead, *Why Coaching Is Becoming So Important* (p. 304).

DISTRIBUTE the handout, *Why Coaching Is Becoming So Important* (p. 181).

REVIEW the exercise and its objectives. Assign breakout rooms, if used.

Leave the definition of coaching open. Encourage participants to think about coaching in ways that are natural to them.

CALL time on the activity and return to the general session.

GROUP DISCUSSION

00:10   **Debrief**

ASK for and answer any questions.

SHOW the overhead, *Changes in Management and Leadership Functions* (p. 290).

Look for and emphasize ideas that suggest managers and leaders are doing:

- Less directing and controlling and more empowering of people.
- Less leading and managing by control and more managing and leading by commitment.

GROUP ACTIVITY

00:20   **What Is Superior Coaching?**

DISTRIBUTE the handout, *What Is Superior Coaching* (p. 183).

REVIEW the exercise and its objectives. Assign breakout rooms, if used.

MAKE the following point:

- Participants should think of their best coaches.

CALL time on the activity and return to the general session.

GROUP DISCUSSION

00:10   **Debrief**

?   *ASK* for and answer any questions.

▣   *MAKE* the following point:

- Look for examples of what superior coaches do and how they do it.

00:10   **Break**

Notes

- _____
- _____
- _____
- _____
- _____
- _____
- _____
- _____
- _____
- _____
- _____
- _____
- _____
- _____
- _____
- _____
- _____
- _____
- _____
- _____

The Superior Coaching Model (Part I)

Purpose   This module of the three-day workshop ensures that participants have a clear understanding of the definition of coaching as portrayed in the Superior Coaching Model and provides participants with a working knowledge of each of the five elements in the model and how they are related.

Workshop Agenda

2. The Superior Coaching Model (Part I)	Minutes 2 hrs 30	Start / Stop 10:00 / 12:30	Actual Start / Stop
Interactive Presentation: The Meaning of Superior Coaching	10	10:00 / 10:10	_____ / _____
(Transition to next topic)	5	10:10 / 10:15	_____ / _____
Interactive Presentation: The Superior Coaching Model	10	10:15 / 10:25	_____ / _____
Understanding the Superior Coaching Model	15	10:25 / 10:40	_____ / _____
Debrief	5	10:40 / 10:45	_____ / _____
(Transition to next topic)	5	10:45 / 10:50	_____ / _____
Clarifying Key Values and Essential Characteristics	35	10:50 / 11:25	_____ / _____
Debrief	10	11:25/ 11:35	_____ / _____
Review/Preview	10	11:35/ 11:45	_____ / _____
Lunch	45	11:45 / 12:30	_____ / _____

Module 2   **The Superior Coaching Model (Part I) (10:00 to 12:30)**

INTERACTIVE PRESENTATION

00:10   **The Meaning of Superior Coaching**

 MAKE the following point:

- Superior coaching is results-oriented and disciplined.

 Trainers should be very familiar with the section, The Meaning of Coaching, in Chapter 2.

 SHOW the overhead, The *Meaning of Superior Coaching* (p. 305).

00:05   **Transition to Superior Coaching Model**

 MAKE the following points:

- It is not just coaches that are important, but superior coaches.

- Superior coaches are disciplined.

- The model is a tool for developing discipline.

INTERACTIVE PRESENTATION

00:10   **Superior Coaching Model**

 MAKE the following point:

- Emphasize that the model is results-oriented.

SHOW the overhead, *The Superior Coaching Model* (p. 306).

DESCRIBE briefly each element in the model:

- Key Values.

- Essential Characteristics.

- Critical Skills.

- Core Conversation.

- Performance Application.

Group Activity

00:15   **Understanding the Superior Coaching Model**

DISTRIBUTE the handout, *Understanding the Superior Coaching Model* (p. 185).

REVIEW the exercise and its objectives. Assign breakout rooms, if used.

MAKE the following point:

- Participants will be using the model in all future activities in the program.

CALL time on the activity and return to the general session.

GROUP DISCUSSION

00:05   **Debrief**

ASK for and answer any questions participants have about the model and its elements. Involve participants in answering the questions.

FACILITATOR COMMENTARY

00:05   **Transition to Clarifying Learning Activities**

MAKE the following points:

- Participants will now look at individual elements in the model.
- Indicate you will examine all elements, but emphasis will be placed on understanding and practicing the critical skills.

GROUP ACTIVITY

00:35   **Clarifying Key Values and Essential Characteristics**

DISTRIBUTE the handout, *Clarifying Key Values and Essential Characteristics* (p. 187).

REVIEW the exercise and its objectives. Assign breakout rooms, if used.

CALL time on the activity and return to the general session.

GROUP DISCUSSION

00:10 **Debrief**

ASK for and answer any questions.

Ensure participants are beginning to see the Superior Coaching Model as a whole and how the individual elements are related to each other.

FACILITATOR COMMENTARY

00:10 **Review/Preview**

SHOW the overhead, *Objectives for Three-Day Workshop* (p. 296) and *REVIEW* those objectives.

SHOW the overhead, *The Meaning of Superior Coaching* (p. 305) and *REVIEW* the meaning.

SHOW the overhead, *The Superior Coaching Model* (p. 306) and *REVIEW* the model.

MAKE the following point:

- The group has been clarifying its understanding of each element in the model.

SHOW the overhead, *Three-Day Program Flow* (p. 301).

MAKE these comments:

After lunch we will:

- Examine the performance applications.

- Take a closer look at the elements of the model.

- Practice using the critical skills.

00:45 **Lunch**

Notes

- _____

- _____

- _____

- _____

- _____

The Superior Coaching Model (Part II)

Purpose   This module of the three-day workshop uses group activities to clarify the critical skills, core conversation, and performance applications of superior coaching.

Workshop Agenda

3. The Superior Coaching Model (Part II)	Minutes 1 hr 45	Start / Stop 12:30 / 2:15	Actual Start / Stop
Clarifying Critical Skills	25	12:30 / 12:55	_____ / _____
Debrief	10	12:55 / 1:05	_____ / _____
Clarifying the Core Conversation	15	1:05 / 1:20	_____ / _____
Debrief	5	1:20 / 1:25	_____ / _____
Clarifying Performance Applications	30	1:25 / 1:55	_____ / _____
Debrief	10	1:55 / 2:05	_____ / _____
Break	10	2:05/ 2:15	_____ / _____

Module 3   **The Superior Coaching Model (Part II) (12:30 to 2:15)**

GROUP ACTIVITY

00:25   **Clarifying Critical Skills**

 DISTRIBUTE the handout, *Clarifying Critical Skills* (p. 191).

 SHOW the overhead, *Critical Skills* (p. 315).

 DESCRIBE briefly each skill:

- Attending.
- Inquiring.
- Reflecting.
- Affirming.
- Being disciplined.

 REVIEW the exercise and its objectives. Assign breakout rooms, if used.

 CALL time on the activity and return to the general session.

GROUP DISCUSSION

00:10   **Debrief**

 ASK for and answer any questions.

GROUP ACTIVITY

00:15   **Clarifying the Core Conversation**

 DISTRIBUTE the handout, *Clarifying the Core Conversation* (p. 196).

 SHOW the overhead, *The Core Conversation* (p. 307).

 MAKE the following point:

- It is important to understand the connection between:
  - Shape as a characteristic of the core conversation.
  - The way shape is developed during a superior coaching conversation.

 REVIEW the exercise and its objectives. Assign breakout rooms, if used.

CALL time on the activity and return to the general session.

GROUP DISCUSSION

00:05   **Debrief**

 ASK for and answer any questions.

MAKE the following points:

- The core conversation is the predictable shape that superior coaching conversations take.

- It is the process of moving from expanding information to focusing the use of this information that makes superior coaching so different from other kinds of coaching conversations.

SHOW the overheads, *The Superior Coaching Model* (p. 306) and *The Core Conversation* (p. 307).

GROUP ACTIVITY

00:30   **Clarifying Performance Applications**

DISTRIBUTE the handout, *Clarifying Performance Applications* (p. 198).

SHOW the overhead, *The Four Performance Applications* (p. 308).

REVIEW the exercise and its objectives. Assign breakout rooms, if used.

CALL time on the activity and return to the general session.

GROUP DISCUSSION

00:10   **Debrief**

ASK for and answer any questions.

MAKE the following point:

- There are many different kinds of coaching conversations, but most pertain to one of the four types of performance applications.

SHOW the overhead, *The Superior Coaching Model* (p. 306).

00:10   **Break**

Values and Beliefs

Purpose

In this module of the three-day workshop, participants learn about the beliefs of superior coaches and identify how these beliefs affect the behavior of superior coaches. Participants are given the opportunity to examine their own beliefs about coaching and compare these to the beliefs of superior coaches.

Workshop Agenda

4. Values and Beliefs	Minutes 1 hr 20	Start / Stop 2:15 / 3:35	Actual Start / Stop
(Transition to next topic)	5	2:15 / 2:20	_____ / _____
What Superior Coaches Believe	35	2:20 / 2:55	_____ / _____
Debrief	10	2:55 / 3:05	_____ / _____
Review and Action Teams Activity	20	3:05 / 3:25	_____ / _____
Review/Preview	10	3:25 / 3:35	_____ / _____

Module 4   **Values and Beliefs (2:15 to 3:35)**

FACILITATOR COMMENTARY

00:05   **Transition to Key Values**

MAKE this comment:

We have been gaining a general overview of the Superior Coaching Model, and now will examine the elements in detail.

GROUP ACTIVITY

00:35   **What Superior Coaches Believe**

DISTRIBUTE the handout, *What Superior Coaches Believe* (p. 200).

SHOW the overhead, *What Superior Coaches Believe* (p. 309).

REVIEW the exercise and its objectives. Assign breakout rooms, if used.

CALL time on the activity and return to the general session.

GROUP DISCUSSION

00:10   **Debrief**

ASK for and answer any questions.

MAKE the following point:

•   Personal beliefs influence one's views of coaching.

Identify specific beliefs.

REVIEW AND ACTION TEAM ACTIVITY

00:20   **Review and Action Logs**

ASK participants to complete a copy of the Review and Action Log to record their key learnings.

If time permits, have each team discuss the key learning points and jointly complete the logs.

FACILITATOR COMMENTARY

00:10   **Review/Preview**

SHOW the overhead, *Objectives for Three-Day Workshop* (p. 296) and *REVIEW* the objectives.

SHOW the overheads, *Changes In Management and Leadership Functions* (p. 290) and *Why Coaching Is Becoming So Important* (p. 304).

REVIEW the key topics covered and the growing importance of coaching as a management and leadership function.

SHOW the overheads, *The Meaning of Superior Coaching* (p. 305) and *The Superior Coaching Model* (p. 306) and *REVIEW* their meaning.

SHOW the overhead, *Three-Day Program Flow* to *PREVIEW* day two.

Notes

- _____
- _____
- _____
- _____
- _____
- _____
- _____
- _____
- _____
- _____
- _____
- _____
- _____
- _____
- _____
- _____
- _____
- _____

Essential Characteristics—Day Two

Purpose

The second day of the three-day workshop gives participants the opportunity to test their understanding of creating balance and identify what superior coaches do to create balance. Participants are given the opportunity to practice using communication that is concrete and that develops shared responsibility.

Objectives

The three-day design provides the best opportunity to develop a good foundation in coaching skills, and, through the use of Review and Action teams, provides the most assurance that what is learned in the training program will improve individual and organizational performance.

Essential Characteristics (Part I)

Purpose

In this module, participants will engage in a group activity to test their understanding of creating balance and to practice being concrete.

Workshop Agenda

1. Essential Characteristics (Part I)	Minutes 2 hrs 35	Start / Stop 8:00 / 10:35	Actual Start / Stop
Introduce Day Two	15	8:00 / 8:15	_____ / _____
(Transition to next topic)	5	8:15 / 8:20	_____ / _____
Testing Our Understanding of Creating Balance	30	8:20 / 8:50	_____ / _____
Debrief	10	8:50 / 9:00	_____ / _____
Practicing Being Concrete	35	9:00 / 9:35	_____ / _____
Debrief	10	9:35 / 9:45	_____ / _____
Practicing Developing Shared Responsibility	35	9:45 / 10:20	_____ / _____
Debrief	5	10:20 / 10:25	_____ / _____
Break	10	10:25 / 10:35	_____ / _____

Module 1   **Essential Characteristics (Part I) (8:00 to 10:45)**

FACILITATOR COMMENTARY

00:15   **Introduce Day Two**

SHOW the overhead, *Three-Day Program Flow* (p. 301) to pre-view what will be covered in Day Two.

ASK for and answer any questions.

00:05   **Transition to Essential Characteristics**

MAKE this comment:

We have looked at the first element in the Superior Coaching Model—key values—and are now looking at the second.

GROUP ACTIVITY

00:30   **Testing Our Understanding of Creating Balance**

DISTRIBUTE the handout, *Testing Our Understanding of Creating Balance* (p. 202).

SHOW the overhead, *The Meaning of Balance* (p. 312).

REVIEW the exercise and its objectives. Assign breakout rooms, if used.

CALL time on the activity and return to the general session.

GROUP DISCUSSION

00:10   **Debrief**

ASK for and answer any questions. Involve participants in answering the questions.

DISCUSS how and what the coach can do to create balance.

GROUP ACTIVITY

00:35   **Practicing Being Concrete**

DISTRIBUTE the handout, *Practicing Being Concrete* (p. 204).

SHOW the overhead, *The Meaning of Being Concrete* (p. 313).

REVIEW the exercise and its objectives. Assign breakout rooms, if used.

CALL time on the activity and return to the general session.

GROUP DISCUSSION

00:10   **Debrief**

ASK for and answer any questions.

ASK participants what behaviors they observed during the exercise that demonstrated lack of being concrete.

GROUP ACTIVITY

00:35   **Practicing Developing Shared Responsibility**

DISTRIBUTE the handout, *Practicing Developing Shared Responsibility* (p. 206).

SHOW the overhead, *Essential Characteristics* (p. 311).

REVIEW the exercise, its objectives and the meaning of shared responsibility. Assign breakout rooms, if used.

CALL time on the activity and return to the general session.

GROUP DISCUSSION

00:05   **Debrief**

ASK for and answer any questions.

ASK participants what behaviors would help develop shared responsibility and behaviors that would not.

00:10   **Break**

Essential Characteristics (Part II)

Purpose   This module of the three-day workshop helps participants test their understanding of the definition of creating shape (the core conversation) and gives them the opportunity to identify communication behaviors that help create shape. Participants practice communicating respect through the behaviors of attending and inquiring and get feedback from their fellow team members.

Workshop Agenda

2. Essential Characteristics (Part II)	Minutes 2 hrs 15	Start / Stop 10:35 / 12:50	Actual Start / Stop
Testing Our Understanding of Creating Shape (The Core Conversation)	30	10:35 / 11:05	_____ / _____
Debrief	10	11:05 / 11:15	_____ / _____
Testing Our Understanding of Communicating Respect	30	11:15 / 11:45	_____ / _____
Debrief	10	11:45 / 11:55	_____ / _____
Review/Preview	10	11:55 / 12:05	_____ / _____
Lunch	45	12:05 / 12:50	_____ / _____

Module 1   **Essential Characteristics (Part II) (10:35 to 12:50)**

GROUP ACTIVITY

00:30   **Testing Our Understanding of Creating Shape
(The Core Conversation)**

 DISTRIBUTE the handout, *Testing Our Understanding of Creating Shape (The Core Conversation)* (p. 209).

 SHOW the overhead, *The Core Conversation* (p. 307).

 MAKE these comments:
- It is important to make the connection between core conversation and shape.
- Shape is an essential characteristic.
- We create shape by using the core conversation.

 REVIEW the exercise and its objectives. Assign breakout rooms, if used.

 CALL time on the activity and return to the general session.

GROUP DISCUSSION

00:10   **Debrief**

 ASK for and answer any questions.

 MAKE the following points:
- It is important to understand shape and relate shape to the core conversation.
- The core conversation is the shape coaches create through their disciplined behaviors.

GROUP ACTIVITY

00:30   **Testing Our Understanding of Communicating Respect**

 DISTRIBUTE the handout, *Practicing Communicating Respect* (p. 217).

 SHOW the overhead, *The Meaning of Respect* (p. 314).

 REVIEW the exercise and its objectives. Assign breakout rooms, if used.

 CALL time on the activity and return to the general session.

GROUP DISCUSSION

00:10   **Debrief**

ASK for and answer any questions.

MAKE the following points:
- Review the list of essential characteristics.
- Review the meaning of respect.

FACILITATOR COMMENTARY

00:10   **Review/Preview**

MAKE this comment:

Emphasis during the morning session has been placed on the essential characteristics identified in the Superior Coaching Model.

SHOW the following overheads to review the characteristics:
- *The Superior Coaching Model* (p. 306).
- *The Core Conversation* (p. 307).
- *Essential Characteristics* (p. 311).
- *The Meaning of Balance* (p. 312).
- *The Meaning of Being Concrete* (p. 313).
- *The Meaning of Respect* (p. 314).

MAKE this comment:

The afternoon session will be concerned with understanding and practicing the critical skills of superior coaching.

00:45   **Lunch**

Notes
- _____
- _____
- _____
- _____
- _____
- _____

Critical Skills

Purpose   This module of the three-day workshop gives participants the opportunity to practice the behaviors of attending, inquiring, reflecting, and affirming. Participants test their understanding of the meaning of respect and receive feedback concerning their performance.

Workshop Agenda

3. Critical Skills	Minutes 2 hrs 50	Start / Stop 12:50 / 3:40	Actual Start / Stop
(Transition to next topic)	5	12:50 / 12:55	_____ / _____
Practicing Attending and Inquiring	35	12:55 / 1:30	_____ / _____
Debrief	10	1:30 / 1:40	_____ / _____
Practicing Reflecting	35	1:40 / 2:15	_____ / _____
Break	10	2:15 / 2:25	
Debrief	10	2:25 / 2:35	_____ / _____
Practicing Affirming	30	2:35 / 3:05	_____ / _____
Debrief	5	3:05 / 3:10	_____ / _____
Review and Action Logs	20	3:10 / 3:30	_____ / _____
Review/Preview	10	3:30 / 3:40	_____ / _____

Module 3   **Critical Skills (12:50 to 3:40)**

FACILITATOR COMMENTARY

00:05   **Transition to Critical Skills**

 SHOW the overheads, *The Superior Coaching Model* (p. 306) and *Critical Skills* (p. 315).

 MAKE these comments:

- We have looked at the first two elements in the Superior Coaching Model—key values and essential characteristics—and are now looking at the third.

- Time does not permit looking at each skill in depth, so we will concentrate on the skills of attending, inquiring, and reflecting.

 Make certain that participants understand each of these skills. Give them concrete illustrations.

GROUP ACTIVITY

00:35   **Practicing Attending and Inquiring**

 DISTRIBUTE the handout, *Practicing Attending and Inquiring* (p. 219).

 SHOW the overhead, *Critical Skills* (p. 315).

 MAKE the following point:

- Emphasize the meaning of attending and inquiring.

 REVIEW the exercise and its objectives. Assign breakout rooms, if used.

 CALL time on the activity and return to the general session.

GROUP DISCUSSION

00:10   **Debrief**

 ASK for and answer any questions. Ask participants for examples of attending and inquiring.

GROUP ACTIVITY

00:45   **Practicing Reflecting**

 DISTRIBUTE the handout, *Practicing Reflecting* (p. 222).

 SHOW the overhead, *Critical Skills* (p. 315).

 REVIEW the exercise and its objectives. Assign breakout rooms, if used.

 CALL time on the activity and return to the general session.

00:10   **Break**

GROUP DISCUSSION

00:10   **Debrief**

 ASK for and answer any questions. Ask participants for examples of reflecting responses to the statements used in the exercise.

GROUP ACTIVITY

00:30   **Practicing Affirming**

 DISTRIBUTE the handout, *Practicing Affirming* (p. 228).

 SHOW the overhead, *Critical Skills* (p. 315).

 REVIEW the exercise, its objectives and the meaning of affirming. Assign breakout rooms, if used.

 CALL time on the activity and return to the general session.

GROUP DISCUSSION

00:05   **Debrief**

 ASK for and answer any questions.

 ASK participants for examples of the three kinds of behavior practiced in the exercise.

REVIEW AND ACTION TEAM ACTIVITY

00:20   **Review and Action Logs**

ASK the Review and Action teams to complete their logs for day two.

If time permits, they can begin to discuss their logs with each other.

FACILITATOR COMMENTARY

00:10   **Review/Preview**

SHOW the overhead, *Objectives for Three-Day Workshop* (p. 296) and **REVIEW** the objectives and what has been covered through day two.

SHOW the overheads, *Essential Characteristics* (p. 311) and *Critical Skills* (p. 315).

MAKE these comments:

- Emphasis during day two has been on the essential characteristics and critical skills of superior coaching.

- Day three will be devoted to the performance applications and two practice interactions.

Indicate which interactions you will be using.

Notes

- _____
- _____
- _____
- _____
- _____
- _____
- _____
- _____
- _____
- _____
- _____
- _____

Resolving Problems—Day Three

Purpose

This module of the three-day workshop gives participants the opportunity to practice all the elements in the Superior Coaching Model and apply the elements to a performance application that focuses on resolving problems. Participants are given feedback on the demonstrated competency in using the Superior Coaching Model and using it in the performance application, *Resolving Problems*.

Workshop Agenda

1. Resolving Problems	Minutes 3 hrs 45	Start / Stop 8:00 / 11:45	Actual Start / Stop
Introduce Day Three	15	8:00 / 8:15	_____ / _____
Review Meaning of Superior Coaching and the Superior Coaching Model	15	8:15 / 8:30	_____ / _____
(Transition to next topic)	5	8:30 / 8:35	_____ / _____
Interactive Presentation— Performance Application: Resolving Problems	15	8:35 / 8:50	_____ / _____
Performance Application: Resolving Problems	2:00	8:50 / 10:50	_____ / _____
Debrief	10	10:50 / 11:00	_____ / _____
Lunch	45	11:00 / 11:45	_____ / _____

Module 1   Resolving Problems (8:00 to 11:45)

FACILITATOR COMMENTARY

00:15   **Introduce Day Three**

 SHOW the overhead, *Objectives for Three-Day Workshop* (p. 296) and *REVIEW* the objectives and what has been covered through day two.

00:15   **Review Meaning of Superior Coaching and the Superior Coaching Model**

 SHOW the overhead, *The Meaning of Superior Coaching* (p. 305).

 MAKE this comment:

Superior coaching is a results-oriented and disciplined process.

 SHOW the overhead, *The Superior Coaching Model* (p. 306).

 MAKE this comment:

The Superior Coaching Model describes a means of creating discipline.

 REVIEW each element in the model and show how the elements are related.

00:05   **Transition to Performance Applications**

 SHOW the overheads, The *Superior Coaching Model* (p. 306) and *The Four Performance Applications* (p. 308).

 MAKE the following points:

- Review the Superior Coaching Model and its elements.

- Emphasize that everything in the model leads to the performance applications, which can make a difference in the performance of individuals and teams.

00:15   **Performance Application: Resolving Problems**

 SHOW the overhead, *Resolving Problems Performance Application* (p. 316).

 DESCRIBE the special characteristics of the resolving problems application. Identify what the coach is accomplishing in the expanding and focusing phases of the conversation.

PRACTICE INTERACTION

02:00   **Performance Application: Resolving Problems**

DISTRIBUTE the handout, *Practice Interaction—Performance Application: Resolving Problems* (p. 232).

SHOW the overhead, *The Four Performance Applications* (p. 308) and *REVIEW* the applications.

SHOW the overhead, *Resolving Problems Performance Applications* (p. 316) and *REVIEW* the applications.

Ensure that the meaning of resolving problems is clear.

GROUP DISCUSSION

00:10   **Debrief**

ASK for and answer any questions and discuss the participants' key learnings.

00:45   **Lunch**

Notes
- _____
- _____
- _____
- _____
- _____
- _____
- _____
- _____
- _____
- _____
- _____
- _____
- _____
- _____
- _____

Skill Practice

Purpose

This module of the three-day workshop allows participants to engage in an interactive presentation and practice interaction based on a performance application of the trainer's choice: *Teaching*, *Supporting Performance*, or *Adjusting Performance*. The session concludes with a review and evaluation of the workshop.

Workshop Agenda

2. Skill Practice	Minutes 3 hrs 40	Start / Stop 11:45 / 3:25	Actual Start / Stop
Review and Action Teams Activity	30	11:45 / 12:15	_____ / _____
Interactive Presentation: Performance Application: Teaching, Supporting Performance, Adjusting Performance (Trainer's choice)	15	12:15 / 12:30	_____ / _____
Performance Application: selected in previous interactive presentation (Trainer's choice)	2:00	12:30 / 2:30	_____ / _____
Debrief	10	2:30 / 2:40	_____ / _____
Review and Action Logs	20	2:40 / 3:00	_____ / _____
Workshop Review and Wrap-up	10	3:00 / 3:10	_____ / _____
Evaluation	15	3:10 / 3:25	_____ / _____

Module 2   Skill Practice (11:45 to 3:25)

00:30   **Review and Action Team Activity**

INTERACTIVE PRESENTATION

00:15   **Performance Application (Trainer's Choice):**
                      Supporting Performance or Adjusting Performance

 SHOW the appropriate overhead:

- *Teaching Performance Application* (p. 318).
- *Supporting Performance Application* (p. 320).
- *Adjusting Performance Application* (p. 322).

 DESCRIBE the special characteristics of the application you selected. Identify what the coach is accomplishing in the expanding and focusing phases of the conversation.

PRACTICE INTERACTION

02:00   **Performance Application (Trainer's Choice)**

 DISTRIBUTE the appropriate handout:

- *Teaching* (p. 239).
- *Supporting Performance* (p. 245).
- *Adjusting Performance* (p. 254).

 SHOW the appropriate overhead:

- *Teaching Performance Application* (p. 318).
- *Supporting Performance Application* (p. 320).
- *Adjusting Performance Application* (p. 322).

 REVIEW the application and ensure that its meaning is clear.

 CALL time on the activity and return to the general session.

GROUP DISCUSSION

00:10   **Debrief**

 ASK for and answer any questions and discuss the participants' key learnings.

REVIEW AND ACTION TEAM ACTIVITY

00:20　　　　　　　　　**Review and Action Logs**

ASK the Review and Action teams to:

- Review their key learnings.

- Refer to the Review and Action logs they completed at the end of day two (or days one and two).

- Complete their logs for day three.

- Discuss their logs.

MAKE the following point if participants are from one organization:

- · Encourage them to commit to a follow-up meeting at a later date to reinforce their learning and support each other's work at becoming superior coaches.

FACILITATOR COMMENTARY

00:10　　　　　　　　　**Workshop Review and Wrap-Up**

SHOW the overhead, *Objectives for Three-Day Workshop* (p. 296) and *REVIEW* the objectives.

SHOW the overheads, *Changes in Management and Leadership Functions* (p. 290), *Why Coaching Is Becoming So Important* (p. 304), and *Three-Day Program Flow* (p. 301).

REVIEW the key topics covered:

- The growing importance of coaching as a management and leadership function.

- The critical skills and performance applications.

SHOW the overheads, *The Meaning of Superior Coaching* (p. 305) and *The Superior Coaching Model* (p. 306).

REVIEW the model and its elements.

INDIVIDUAL ACTIVITY

00:15　　　　　　　　　**Evaluation**

DISTRIBUTE the *Workshop Evaluation—Long Form* to each participant (p. 275).

Chapter Nine:

Learning Activities

There are three kinds of learning activities in this chapter:

- Exercises.

- Learning Transfer Tools.

- Program Evaluation Forms.

Where each of the learning activities is used in each of the coaching training workshops has been identified in Chapters 4 to 8.

USING THE LEARNING ACTIVITIES

You may use the learning activities in two ways:

- Key them into your word processing system "as is" or customize them to suit your specific needs.
- Photocopy the learning activities that you need from this book and use them "as is."

TRAINER'S NOTES

Using the Exercises

Exercises in this section have been organized in the following five ways:

1. All are generally in the same sequence that they are used in a coaching skills program. In other words, the first exercises in this section will be those you most likely use in the early part of a program, and the later ones will be those you will typically use in the later part of a program.

2. All are based on the definition of coaching presented in Chapter 2.

> ## SUPERIOR COACHING
>
> Superior coaching is a disciplined conversation, using concrete performance information, between a leader and an individual or a team that results in the continuous improvement of performance.

3. All follow the same format:

   - Each is designed as either a handout or as a page in a notebook you assemble for participants.

   - We have recommended times listed for each exercise, but times will change based on the number of participants in a program, the number of participants working as teams, and your own style. Therefore, a blank ("You have ___ minutes for this exercise.") is provided for your customization.

   - Each has a set of objectives that describes the outcomes expected.

   - Each lists the tasks that participants are expected to perform and the order in which they are to be performed.

   - Each has two parts: *Trainer's Notes* and a *Handout* for each participant.

4. A short set of instructions for setting up and debriefing each exercise is included in the section of each design described in Chapters 4 to 8. They give a basic idea of the content of each design and a tool for general planning. The Trainer's Notes, however, are more detailed. Refer to these notes until you have repeated the exercises several times and become thoroughly familiar with them.

5. We have indicated the approximate amount of time required for each exercise. It is not possible to indicate exactly how long an exercise will take, which depends on the:

- Number of members at each table.

- Number of participants present.

- Amount of importance the trainer places on the exercise.

Notes

- _____

- _____

- _____

- _____

- _____

- _____

- _____

- _____

- _____

- _____

- _____

- _____

- _____

- _____

- _____

- _____

- _____

- _____

- _____

- _____

- _____

- _____

- _____

- _____

How the Jobs of Leading and Managing Are Changing and Why

Objectives

To develop a picture of how the roles of managing and leading have been changing over the past few years, and to develop a consensus about the most important changes.

Description

Coaching has always been a characteristic function of the best managers and leaders. Today, however, the coaching function is becoming a critical function of managers and leaders as companies downsize, reduce the function of direct supervision, and use teams and teamwork as primary organizing principles. This exercise helps sensitize participants to the growing importance of coaching and to see it as a primary competency for managers and leaders at every level.

Time

- 25 minutes.

Materials

- Copy of *How the Jobs of Leading and Managing Are Changing and Why* for each participant (p. 179).

- Overhead, *Changes in Management and Leadership Functions* (p. 290).

- Chapter 2, *COACHING: The ASTD Trainer's Sourcebook.*

Directions

1. Review the exercise and its objectives.

2. Assign breakout rooms, if used.

3. Assign time to complete exercise and return to general session.

4. Remind participants to think concretely about their own experiences as leaders or as observers of leaders in their own organizations.

Debrief

Make sure the following ideas are brought out:

 Control model of managing is disappearing.

 Coaching function is becoming a critical function of managers and leaders as companies downsize, reduce the function of direct supervision, and use teams and teamwork as primary organizing principles.

<u>HANDOUT</u>

How the Jobs of Leading and Managing Are Changing and Why

Time   You have _____ minutes for this exercise.

Objectives   To develop a picture of how the roles of managing and leading have been changing over the past few years and to develop a consensus about the most important changes.

Directions   1. Review this exercise as a team and ensure that your team understands what tasks it must complete.

2. Work individually and think about ways that the role of managers and leaders has changed over the past few years. In the first column below jot down a few notes about what you believe managers and leaders are doing less of now than they were five or ten years ago. In the second column jot down a few notes about what you think managers and leaders are doing more of today than they were five or ten years ago.

Doing less of . . .	Doing more of . . .

3. Work as a team. Appoint a recorder. Discuss what each person has noted from Step 2. On chart paper, list the ways that functions of managing and leading have changed.

4. Review your list from Step 3. Select two or three things that managers and leaders are doing less of and two or three things that they are now doing more—those things your team feels are most important.

5. Bring the results from Step 4 for discussion at the general session.

TRAINER'S NOTES	# Why Coaching Is Becoming So Important

Objectives

To clarify the place that coaching has in the changing role of managing and leading and increase awareness of the importance of coaching.

Description

This exercise helps participants relate coaching to performance and to connect coaching with the process of improving the performance of individuals and teams.

Time

- 20 minutes.

Materials

- Copy of *Why Coaching Is Becoming So Important* for each participant (p. 181).

- Overhead, *Why Coaching Is Becoming So Important* (p. 304).

- Overhead, *Changes in Management and Leadership Functions* (p. 290).

- Chapter 1, *COACHING: The ASTD Trainer's Sourcebook*.

Directions

1. Review the exercise and its objectives.

2. Assign breakout rooms, if used.

3. Assign time to complete exercise and return to general session.

4. At this point in the program leave the definition of coaching open. Encourage participants to think about coaching in the ways that are natural to them.

Debrief   ☑

Look for and emphasize ideas that suggest managers and leaders are doing:

- Less directing and controlling and more empowering of people.

- Less leading and managing by control and more managing and leading by commitment.

☑   Chapter 1 is a resource for debriefing this exercise.
Use overhead, *Changes in Management and Leadership Functions* (p. 290).

<u>H</u>ANDOUT	**Why Coaching Is Becoming So Important**

Time

You have _____ minutes for this exercise.

Objectives

To clarify the place that coaching has in the changing role of managing and leading and to increase awareness of the importance of coaching.

Directions

1. Review this exercise as a team and ensure that your team understands what tasks it must complete.

2. Work as a team. Appoint a recorder. Discuss the following questions:

   • "From what you already know about coaching, how do you think coaching fits into the changing role of managing and leading?"

   • "What may make coaching more important today than it has been in the past?"

3. Record your team's conclusions on chart paper.

4. Bring your conclusions from Step 3 to the general session.

TRAINER'S NOTES

What Is Superior Coaching?

Objectives

To clarify the definition of coaching and increase awareness of the definition of superior coaching.

Description

This exercise begins to build the basis for the idea of superior coaching. Participants can identify from their own experiences those leaders who have been good coaches and those who have not. Their experience can give credibility to the definition of superior coaching that is developed later, and the Superior Coaching Model.

Time

- 20 minutes.

Materials

- Copy of *What Is Superior Coaching?* for each participant (p. 183).

Directions

1. Review the exercise and its objectives.

2. Assign breakout rooms, if used.

3. Assign time to complete exercise and return to general session.

4. Emphasize that participants are to think of their *best* coaches.

Debrief   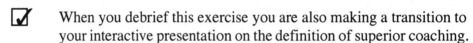 When you debrief this exercise you are also making a transition to your interactive presentation on the definition of superior coaching.

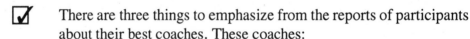 There are three things to emphasize from the reports of participants about their best coaches. These coaches:

1. Accomplished something—they improved performance.

2. Performed a variety of functions:

   - Resolving problems.
   - Teaching.
   - Supporting.
   - Challenging.
   - Adjusting.

3. Were disciplined in the way they interacted.

<u>H</u>ANDOUT	**What Is Superior Coaching?**

Time

You have _____ minutes for this exercise.

Objectives

To clarify the definition of coaching and increase awareness of the definition of superior coaching.

Directions

1. Review this exercise as a team and ensure that your team understands what tasks it must complete.

2. Think of a coach as someone who periodically has conversations with others and is able to help others improve their performance by teaching them new skills, or helping them solve problems, or challenging them to take on more difficult tasks and jobs. Work individually and think about the best coach that you can remember from your work experience. Jot down a few notes about why you remember the person as such a good coach.

3. Work as a team. Appoint a recorder. Discuss what each person has noted from Step 2. Develop a profile of what your team thinks a good or superior coach does.

4. Bring the profile developed in Step 3 to the general session.

5. Based on your discussions in Step 3, review the definition of superior coaching found below. What would you add to the definition based on the profile you developed in Step 3? Bring the results of this task to the general session.

SUPERIOR COACHING

Superior coaching is a disciplined conversation, using concrete performance information, that takes place between a leader and an individual or a team that results in the continuous improvement of performance.

Trainer's Notes	# Understanding the Superior Coaching Model

Objectives

To ensure that participants have a clear understanding of the definition of coaching as portrayed in the Superior Coaching Model, and to ensure participants have a working knowledge of each of the five elements in the model and how they are related.

Description

This exercise gives participants the chance to discuss with each other the Superior Coaching Model, to clarify the definition of each element in the model, and to identify unresolved questions about the model.

Time

- 15 minutes.

Materials

- Copy of *Understanding The Superior Coaching Model* for each participant (p. 185).

- Overhead, *The Meaning of Superior Coaching* (p. 305).

- Overhead, *The Superior Coaching Model* (p. 306).

- Chapter 2, *COACHING: The ASTD Trainer's Sourcebook.*

Directions

1. Review the exercise and its objectives.

2. Assign breakout rooms, if used.

3. Assign time to complete exercise and return to general session.

4. Keep the overhead of the Superior Coaching Model on screen during the exercise.

5. Remind participants that they will be using the model in all future activities in the program.

Debrief

☑ Field any questions that participants have about the model. Involve participants in answering the questions.

☑ Keep overhead, *The Superior Coaching Model,* on screen.

<u>H</u>ANDOUT	**Understanding the Superior Coaching Model**

Time

You have _____ minutes for this exercise.

Objectives

To ensure that participants have a clear understanding of the definition of coaching as portrayed in the Superior Coaching Model and to ensure participants have a working knowledge of each of the five elements in the model and how they are related.

Directions

1. Review this exercise as a team and ensure that your team understands what tasks it must complete.

2. Have each person work independently and spend a few moments reviewing the Superior Coaching Model. Note any questions that you have about the model, its elements, and how they are related.

3. Have one team member volunteer to give his/her understanding of the model and how it describes superior coaching. Ask other members to add anything they feel might help further clarify the model.

4. Review any questions that members noted about the model in Steps 2 and 3. Have a team member record any questions about the model that the team would like to have discussed in the general session. Bring these questions to the general session.

TRAINER'S NOTES	# Clarifying Key Values and Essential Characteristics

Objectives

To help participants clarify the first two elements in the Superior Coaching Model—key values and essential characteristics—and prepare themselves to use these elements in later exercises.

Description

Superior coaching is graphically defined in the Superior Coaching Model. The model has five elements:

- Key values.

- Essential characteristics.

- Critical skills.

- Core conversation.

- Performance applications.

This exercise begins to clarify for participants the definition of key values and essential characteristics by having each individual read descriptions of these elements and then select a topic relevant to key values and essential characteristics and coach other team members on these topics.

Time

- 35 minutes.

Materials

- Copy of *Clarifying Key Values and Essential Characteristics* for each participant (p. 187).

- Overhead, *The Superior Coaching Model* (p. 306).

- Chapter 2, *COACHING: The ASTD Trainer's Sourcebook*.

Directions

1. Review the exercise and its objectives.

2. Assign breakout rooms, if used.

3. Assign time to complete exercise and return to general session.

4. Refer to the Superior Coaching Model in setting up the exercise. Make certain that participants know where they are in developing their understanding of each element in the model.

Debrief   ☑

Ensure participants are beginning to see the Superior Coaching Model as a whole and how the individual elements are related to each other.

☑

Keep the overhead, *The Superior Coaching Model*, on screen.

<u>H</u>ANDOUT	**Clarifying Key Values and Essential Characteristics**
Time	You have _____ minutes for this exercise.
Objectives	To help participants clarify the first two elements in the Superior Coaching Model—key values and essential characteristics—and prepare themselves to use these elements in later exercises.

Directions

1. Review this exercise as a team and ensure that your team understands what tasks it must complete.

2. Each person work independently and spend a few moments reviewing the definitions of key values and essential characteristics that follow. Each person should be able to describe these two elements in their own words.

3. Assign or have each person select one of the topics listed below and "coach" the team about the definition of the topic. You may not have enough people for all topics. If you have more topics than people, assign a few members two topics. Limit each person's coaching session to three minutes per topic.

   • How does what managers and leaders believe about people's competency and their need for competency affect what managers and leaders do about coaching?

   • What conditions at work tend to build commitment in people?

   • How can coaching help build commitment?

   • What do superior coaches typically believe about opportunities for coaching?

   • What makes a "disciplined" coach different from other people who try to coach?

   • What is meant by the term "essential characteristics"?

   • What is the meaning of "balance"?

   • What is the meaning of "being concrete"?

   • What is the meaning of "shared responsibility"?

   • What is the meaning of "shape"?

   • What is the meaning of "respect"?

4. Review your experience in Step 3. If your team has any questions about the meaning of key values and essential characteristics, bring these questions to the general session.

Key Values and Essential Characteristics

Key values

Superior coaches are managers and leaders who share certain kinds of beliefs about:

- Human competency.

- How people committed to superior performance are developed.

- The value of coaching.

They believe:

- People want to be competent and, given the necessary help, will strive to become more competent.

- People must be given the opportunity to demonstrate their competency for them to continue to become more competent.

- Managing by control is not practical and does not lead to people being committed to superior performance and the continuous improvement of performance.

- Superior performance results from the commitment of individuals and teams to be superior.

- They must initiate coaching interactions and use every interaction with individuals and teams as a potential opportunity to coach—rather than direct.

- That to be a superior coach they must be disciplined.

Essential characteristics

Positive results from coaching interactions require that coaches:

- Create an environment conducive to learning.

- Use the set of superior coaching skills.

- Create the structure of the core coaching conversation which underlies superior coaching.

- Apply the skills and core conversation to specific opportunities for continuous improvement of performance.

The logic is that the superior coach moves from his/her internal set of values into learning all that it takes to be a superior coach:

- Creating the essential characteristics.

- Learning to use the critical skills.

- Learning to use the skills to create the core conversation.

- Applying all this to various performance applications.

Five Essential Characteristics

Five characteristics distinguish a superior coaching conversation from other conversations. Superior coaches use disciplined behavior and aim to create it in others by example. Look for the following specific qualities of superior coaching.

Balance

Superior coaching is not one-sided. There is give and take, a questioning and sharing of information and ideas with the full involvement of all parties.

Being concrete

Superior coaching uses language that is to the point and encourages the persons being coached to be specific. It focuses on the objective and descriptive aspects of performance.

Shared responsibility

Both the coach and the persons being coached have a shared responsibility to work together for the continuous improvement of performance. All participants in a coaching conversation share the responsibility for making that conversation as useful as possible, and for the continuous improvement of performance that follows the conversation.

Shape

Superior coaching has a distinctive shape that can be reproduced over and over again. The shape, as shown below, is determined by these important factors:

- The goal of the coaching conversation is clearly stated.

- The flow of the conversation expands information and then focuses the information as the participants move toward the goal.

Respect

A final qualitative characteristic of superior coaching is that the leader communicates respect for the people being coached. Demonstrating respect uses behaviors in a conversation which involve the other person and make that person a fully accepted player.

TRAINER'S NOTES	**Clarifying Critical Skills**

Objectives

To help participants clarify the third element in the Superior Coaching Model—critical skills—and prepare them to use this element in later exercises.

Description

Superior coaching is graphically defined in the Superior Coaching Model. The model has five elements:

- Key values.

- Essential characteristics.

- Critical skills.

- Core conversation.

- Performance applications.

This exercise begins to clarify for participants the definition of critical skills by having each individual read descriptions of the skills and then coach other team members on the definition of one or more of these skills.

Time

- 25 minutes.

Materials

- Copy of *Clarifying Critical Skills* for each participant (p. 191).

- Overhead, *The Superior Coaching Model* (p. 306).

- Overhead, *Critical Skills* (p. 315).

- Chapter 2, *COACHING: The ASTD Trainer's Sourcebook.*

Directions

1. Review the exercise and its objectives.

2. Assign breakout rooms, if used.

3. Assign time to complete exercise and return to general session.

4. Overhead *Critical Skills* (p. 315) lists the critical skills. Show this overhead and describe briefly each of the skills as you introduce this exercise.

Debrief

☑ Field questions.

☑ Ensure participants are beginning to see the Superior Coaching Model as a whole and how the individual elements are related to each other.

☑ Keep the overhead, *The Superior Coaching Model*, on screen.

<u>H</u>ANDOUT	**Clarifying Critical Skills**

Time

You have _____ minutes for this exercise.

Objectives

To help participants clarify the third element in the Superior Coaching Model—critical skills—and prepare them to use this element in later exercises.

Directions

1. Review this exercise as a team and ensure that your team understands what tasks it must complete.

2. Assign each member one of the critical skills. Some skills will be assigned more than once and repeated among team members. Repetition is useful.

   The skills are:

   • Attending.

   • Inquiring.

   • Reflecting.

   • Affirming.

   • Being disciplined.

3. Each person read the relevant description of the core skills below and coach the team on the skill assigned. Limit coaching sessions to three minutes.

ATTENDING

The term attending refers to the vocal and nonvocal techniques used by coaches to convey active listening. Nonvocal behaviors include:

• Facing the other person.

• Keeping comfortable eye contact.

• Nodding in agreement.

• Avoiding distracting behaviors such as fidgeting, thumbing through papers, and interrupting.

The nonvocal aspects of attending encourage the other person to interact easily and to develop the necessary information. Vocal responses such as "Uh huh," "Yes," "I can see that," "OK," etc., communicate to the other person that the coach is paying attention.

INQUIRING

Another key to superior coaching is to develop sufficient information so positive results can be achieved. Inquiring is a set of behaviors that helps develop information.

Inquiring takes the following forms:

- **Questions**

  "So what did you do when you learned the contractor was going to be late completing the first phase?"

- **Directives**

  "Tell me what you did when you learned the contractor was going to be late completing the first phase."

Questions and directives may be closed or open. A closed question might be, "Should Jones be included on the team?" An open question might be, "What sort of people do you think we should put on the team?" A closed directive might be, "Tell me how long it will take for you to complete the plan." An open directive might be, "Tell me what you think you must do to complete the plan."

REFLECTING

Reflecting is a behavior by which coaches communicate that they:

- Are listening.

- Understand what the other person is saying and/or feeling.

- Have suspended judgment.

- Want the other person to develop information that is important to that person.

Reflecting is not mirroring or repeating verbatim what the other person has said. It is playing back to the other person what the coach believes has been said, and/or communicating the feelings that the other person has conveyed as shown in the following examples:

Other: "It just isn't possible to get the contractor to respond. He has it in his head that he works for his corporate headquarters and not for me."

Coach: "So, you feel almost powerless to get him to do the job you think he should."

Other: "I don't see how I can keep putting my people on all these *Total Quality Management* (T.Q.M.) teams. I have just enough people to manage our trouble calls. If they are all on teams, it's me that's going to get the flak when somebody has a computer down. My customers don't care about my problems."

Coach: "The way you see it at the moment is that you're in a no-win situation. Management wants you to participate in its T.Q.M. program, but to you that means you may disappoint your customers."

AFFIRMING

Affirming reinforces the sense of competency in the other person and contributes directly to that person's commitment to continuous improvement.

Affirming during a coaching interaction may draw attention to two sets of competencies that the other person has demonstrated: First, those competencies which the person has demonstrated on the job; second, those competencies that the person demonstrates during a coaching interaction. Here are a couple of examples:

- **Teaching**

  "I know it was tough for you to spend so much time learning the new accounting system, and I know it hasn't been easy having these sessions with me to help you get up to speed in a hurry. You have really done a fine job."

- **Resolving Problems**

  "Thanks for the way you've tried to resolve this problem with your team. It has been very helpful to me to understand better just what issues you all face."

BEING DISCIPLINED

Being disciplined means, at the least:

- Assuming responsibility for one's own behavior and accepting the responsibility for the outcome of a coaching interaction. It is the clearheaded and responsible approach which says, "If it didn't turn out so well, I had something to do with it," and "If it did turn out well, I had something to do with it."

- Understanding and being committed to creating the essential characteristics of superior coaching during every coaching interaction.

It means understanding and being committed to creating the general shape of every superior coaching conversation.

Review

☑ **Review the Superior Coaching Model**

Discuss as a team how the first three elements—key values, essential characteristics, and critical skills—are related to each other and to superior coaching.

☑ **Review experience as a team**

Review your experience working as a team in this exercise. Bring any questions your team has to the general session.

Clarifying the Core Conversation

Objectives

To help participants clarify the core conversation element in the Superior Coaching Model, and prepare to use this element in later exercises.

Description

This exercise continues to clarify the elements in the Superior Coaching Model and addresses the definition of the fourth element in the model, core conversation. Participants discuss the definition of core conversation and bring any questions they have to the general session.

Time

- 15 minutes.

Materials

- Copy of *Clarifying the Core Conversation* for each participant (p. 196).

- Overhead, *The Superior Coaching Model* (p. 306).

- Overhead, *The Core Conversation* (p. 307).

- Chapter 2, *COACHING: The ASTD Trainer's Sourcebook*.

Directions

1. Review the exercise and its objectives.

2. Assign breakout rooms, if used.

3. Assign time to complete exercise and return to general session.

4. Review the overhead, *The Core Conversation*. Ensure connection is made between shape as a characteristic and the core conversation the way shape is developed during a superior coaching conversation. Leave the overhead on screen during the exercise.

Debrief

Make the following points:

☑ The core conversation is the predictable shape that superior coaching conversations take.

☑ Emphasize that it is the process of moving from expanding information to focusing the use of this information that makes superior coaching so different from other kinds of coaching conversations.

<u>H</u>ANDOUT	**Clarifying the Core Conversation**

Time

You have _____ minutes for this exercise.

Objectives

To help participants clarify the core conversation element in the Superior Coaching Model, and prepare to use this element in later exercises.

Directions

1. Review this exercise as a team and ensure that your team understands what tasks it must complete.

2. Review as a team the model of the core conversation. Discuss the following questions:

    •   What is the expanding phase and the focusing phase in the model and how are they related?

    •   How are the essential characteristics related to the expanding phase of coaching? If these characteristics are not present, how is the expanding phase affected?

    •   How are the essential characteristics related to the focusing phase of coaching? If these characteristics are not present, how is the focusing phase affected?

    •   How are the critical skills related to the expanding phase of coaching? If these skills are not used, how is the expanding phase affected?

    •   How are the critical skills related to the focusing phase of coaching? If these skills are not used, how is the focusing phase affected?

3. Review as a team your experience in this exercise. Bring any questions your team has to the general session.

<u>TRAINER'S NOTES</u>	**Clarifying Performance Applications**

Objectives

To help participants clarify performance applications in the Superior Coaching Model and prepare to use this element in later exercises.

Description

In this exercise, participants clarify the final element in the Superior Coaching Model, performance applications. They work as teams and review each of the four major coaching performance applications. They then draw the outline of the core conversation on their flip charts and show what would happen in the expanding and focusing phases for each of the performance applications.

Time

- 30 minutes.

Materials

- Copy of *Clarifying Performance Applications* for each participant (p. 198).

- Overhead, *The Superior Coaching Model* (p. 306).

- Overhead, *The Four Performance Applications* (p. 308).

- Chapter 2, *COACHING: The ASTD Trainer's Sourcebook.*

Directions

1. Review the exercise and its objectives.

2. Assign breakout rooms, if used.

3. Assign time to complete exercise and return to general session.

4. Review overhead, *The Four Performance Applications*. Leave the overhead on screen during the exercise.

Debrief

Make certain participants understand that there are many, many different kinds of coaching conversations, but most of them fall into the four types identified:

- Resolving Problems.

- Teaching.

- Supporting Performance.

- Adjusting Performance.

<u>HANDOUT</u>	**Clarifying Performance Applications**

Time

You have _____ minutes for this exercise.

Objectives

To help participants clarify performance applications in the Superior Coaching Model and prepare to use this element in later exercises.

Directions

1. Review this exercise as a team and ensure that your team understands what tasks it must complete.

2. Work as a team. Review each of the four major coaching performance applications and ensure that team members understand each application. Draw the outline of the core conversation on your flip charts. As you discuss each application, give concrete examples of the possible content of such conversations based on your experience. Fill in the areas of the two phases of the core conversation on your flip charts with what sort of things you would try to accomplish and what sort of skills you would use in each phase and for each application. The four major performance applications of coaching are:

   • Resolving problems.

   • Teaching new knowledge or skills.

   • Supporting performance.

   • Adjusting performance.

3. Bring one example from Step 2 to the general session.

4. Review your experience from this exercise and bring any questions about the performance applications in the Superior Coaching Model to the general session.

TRAINER'S NOTES	**What Superior Coaches Believe**

Objectives

To help participants understand the beliefs of superior coaches and identify how these beliefs affect the behavior of superior coaches. Participants are given the opportunity to examine their own beliefs about coaching and compare these to the beliefs of superior coaches.

Description

Participants work as teams and review the beliefs that are characteristic of superior coaches. (They may have already briefly reviewed these beliefs in another exercise.) In this exercise, however, they associate specific implications listed below and ensure each team member understands them. They should work as a team. For each belief identified in Step 2, they will identify at least one concrete implication of the belief, i.e., something specific that a coach would do because of the belief. Space has been provided under each belief for their notes.

Time

- 35 minutes.

Materials

- Copy of *What Superior Coaches Believe* for each participant (p. 200).

- Overhead, *The Superior Coaching Model* (p. 306).

- Overhead, *What Superior Coaches Believe* (p. 309).

- Chapter 2, *COACHING: The ASTD Trainer's Sourcebook.*

Directions

1. Review the exercise and its objectives.

2. Assign breakout rooms, if used.

3. Assign time to complete exercise and return to general session.

4. Review the overhead, *What Superior Coaches Believe.* Leave the overhead on screen during the exercise.

Debrief

☑ Field questions.

☑ Discuss how beliefs influence what coaches actually do.

☑ Show how the beliefs of superior coaches influence what they do.

<u>HANDOUT</u>	**What Superior Coaches Believe**
Time	You have _____ minutes for this exercise.
Objectives	To help participants understand the beliefs of superior coaches and identify how these beliefs affect the behavior of superior coaches. Participants are given the opportunity to examine their own beliefs about coaching and compare these to the beliefs of superior coaches.
Directions	1. Review this exercise as a team and ensure all members understand what tasks they must complete.
	2. Work as a team. Review the beliefs that are characteristic of superior coaches listed below and ensure each team member understands them.
	3. Work as a team. For each belief identified in Step 2, identify at least one concrete implication of the belief, i.e., something specific that a coach would do because of the belief. Space has been provided under each belief for your notes.
	4. Bring the results from Step 3 to the general session.
	5. Examine your beliefs about coaching and note where they might be tested or examined further.

- People want to be competent, and, given the necessary help, will strive to become more so.

- People must be given the opportunity to demonstrate their competency on a continual basis.

- Managing by control is not practical and does not lead to a commitment to or the continuous improvement of superior performance.

- Superior performance results from the commitment of individuals and teams to perform at the best of their ability.

- Superior coaches believe they must initiate coaching interactions and use every interaction with individuals and teams as a potential opportunity to coach—rather than to direct.

- Superior coaches believe in discipline.

TRAINER'S NOTES	**Testing Our Understanding of Creating Balance**

Objectives

To help participants test their understanding of the definition of balance and identify what superior coaches do to create balance.

Description

Participants work as teams and review the definition of balanced. They then identify the ways that coaches might create imbalance in a coaching interaction, i.e., the coach tends to do too much talking, or the person being coached does too much talking. Next they identify ways that coaches might create balance in a coaching interaction, i.e., both the coach and the person being coached mutually contribute to the coaching conversation.

Time

- 30 minutes.

Materials

- Copy of *Testing Our Understanding of Creating Balance* for each participant (p. 202).

- Overhead, *The Superior Coaching Model* (p. 306).

- Overhead, *Meaning of Balance* (p. 312).

- Chapter 2, *COACHING: The ASTD Trainer's Sourcebook*.

Directions

1. Review the exercise and its objectives.

2. Assign breakout rooms, if used.

3. Assign time to complete exercise and return to general session.

4. Review the overhead, *Meaning of Balance*. Leave the overhead on screen during the exercise.

Debrief

☑ Field any questions that participants have about balance. Involve participants in answering the questions.

☑ Keep the overhead, *Meaning of Balance*, on the screen.

☑ Help participants understand the value of balance, and what the coach can do to create balance.

<u>H</u>ANDOUT	**Testing Our Understanding of Creating Balance**

Time

You have _____ minutes for this exercise.

Objectives

To help participants test their understanding of the definition of balance and identify what superior coaches do to create balance.

Directions

1. Review this exercise as a team and ensure that your team understands what tasks it must complete.

2. Review as a team the following definition of balance and ensure that each member understands the definition.

BALANCE

Superior coaching is not one-sided. There is a give and take, questioning, sharing of information and ideas, all parties are fully involved. Balance is what a superior coach creates through skilled and disciplined behavior.

---

3. Work as a team. Select a recorder. Identify as many ways as you can that coaches might create imbalance in a coaching interaction, i.e., the coach tends to do too much talking, or the person being coached does too much talking. Record your results for discussion in the general session.

4. Identify as many ways as you can that coaches might create balance in a coaching interaction, i.e., both the coach and the person being coached mutually contribute to the coaching conversation. Record your results for discussion in the general session.

<u>TRAINER'S NOTES</u>	**Practicing Being Concrete**

Objectives   To give participants the opportunity to practice using communication that is concrete and get feedback from their fellow team members.

Description   In this exercise participants practice making a concrete statement to their fellow team members and receive feedback about just how concrete their statements were. They then have the opportunity to make their statements more concrete.

Time
- 35 minutes.

Materials
- A copy of *Practicing Being Concrete* for each participant (p. 204).

- Overhead, *Meaning of Being Concrete* (p. 313).

- Chapter 2, *COACHING: The ASTD Trainer's Sourcebook.*

Directions
1. Review the exercise and its objectives.

2. Assign breakout rooms, if used.

3. Assign time to complete exercise and return to general session.

4. Review overhead, *Meaning of Being Concrete*. Leave the overhead on screen during the exercise.

Debrief   ☑   Field questions.

☑   Ask participants what behaviors they observed during the exercise that demonstrated a lack of being concrete.

<u>HANDOUT</u>	**Practicing Being Concrete**
Time	You have _____ minutes for this exercise.
Objectives	To give participants the opportunity to practice using communication that is concrete and get feedback from their fellow team members.

Directions

1. Review this exercise as a team and ensure that your team understands what tasks it must complete.

2. Have each team member select from the list below one coaching opportunity for which he/she would like to make a concrete statement as a coach to his/her fellow team members. Write down the statement.

    •   Describe to your team at least one way that it could improve its performance for the remainder of the program.

    •   Describe to your team what you think are the two most important characteristics of superior teams.

    •   Describe to your team what you think is the most important skill for being a superior coach.

    •   Describe to your team what you think are the team's strengths.

3. Read Steps 3 and 4 before proceeding because they take place together. Each person reads his/her statement from Step 2 to the team, after which each team member gives feedback based on the following questions:

    •   What part of the statement was clearly concrete, i.e., immediately understood?

    •   What part of the statement was insufficiently concrete, i.e., not immediately understood?

    •   What should the person change to make his/her statement more concrete?

4. When you are receiving feedback from your fellow team members in Step 3, take notes. After each person has given you feedback, indicate how the person might have been more concrete in the feedback, i.e., more immediately understood.

5. Discuss your experience in this exercise and bring any questions to the general session.

<u>Trainer's Notes</u>	# Practicing Developing Shared Responsibility

Objectives
To give participants the opportunity to practice communication behaviors that develop shared responsibility and get feedback from their fellow team members.

Description
Each participant is assigned a mini case. Each member prepares something to say during the coaching discussion described in the mini cases to help develop the proper degree of shared responsibility. After each member practices developing shared responsibility, other team members provide feedback.

Time
- 35 minutes.

Materials
- Copy of *Practicing Developing Shared Responsibility* for each participant (p. 206).

- Overhead, *Essential Characteristics* (p. 311).

- Chapter 2, *COACHING: The ASTD Trainer's Sourcebook.*

Directions
1. Review the exercise and its objectives.

2. Assign breakout rooms, if used.

3. Assign time to complete exercise and return to general session.

4. Review the overhead, *Essential Characteristics*.

5. Review the definition of shared responsibility.

Debrief   Field questions.

 Mention behaviors from the exercise that help develop shared responsibility and those that do not.

<u>H</u>ANDOUT   **Practicing Developing Shared Responsibility**

Time   You have _____ minutes for this exercise.

Objectives   To give participants the opportunity to practice communication behaviors that develop shared responsibility and get feedback from their fellow team members.

Directions

1. Review this exercise as a team and ensure that your team understands what tasks it must complete.

2. Assign the following mini cases in order to team members. If your team is large, assign more than one person to the same case. Each member prepares something that he/she might say during the coaching discussion described in the mini cases to help develop the proper degree of shared responsibility with the other person(s).

3. Each person reads his/her statement from Step 2 to the team. After each person reads the statement, each person on the team gives feedback around the following questions:

   • Was some idea of shared responsibility communicated?

   • Did the coach assume too much responsibility?

   • Did the coach try to give the other person(s) too much responsibility?

   • How might the statement that the coach made be improved?

 When you receive feedback from your colleagues, you don't have to accept it, but try to use it. Make sure you understand it first, then file it for possible use to improve the creation of shared responsibility.

4. Discuss your experience in this exercise and bring any questions to the general session.

Mini cases

Case A

You have an employee who persistently makes grammatical mistakes in written reports. The employee is working on a report analyzing plans for office automation. You have reviewed a draft and found several incomplete sentences, non-agreement in subjects and verbs, and mistakes in punctuation. You have called the employee in to discuss the problem.

Case B

You have stopped by the office of one of your employees as part of your "walking around" strategy. You ask the employee, "How are things going?" The employee says, "I don't think I am going to meet the planned schedule for the next design review."

Case C

The results of a recent organizational survey show that the people in your work group have a low commitment to doing their best all the time. You have called a team meeting to discuss the problem.

Case D

Your work group is required to submit weekly notes describing major activities, problems, and achievements to senior management. You have an employee who regularly fails to prepare those notes on time. You are in the midst of a coaching conversation to adjust the employee's performance.

Case E

You have an employee who never volunteers for tough or dirty jobs, and rarely assists other work group members when they need help. Others' impressions are that the employee is willing to do only the minimum amount of work to get by and has little commitment to doing superior work. You are discussing the problem with the employee.

<u>TRAINER'S NOTES</u>

Testing Our Understanding of Creating Shape (The Core Conversation)

Objectives

To help participants test their understanding of the definition of creating shape (the core conversation) and to give them the opportunity to identify communication behaviors that help create shape.

Description

In this exercise participants work as teams and review the definition of creating shape (the core conversation). Next, each member selects a mini case, and imagines having a coaching conversation using the case. The core conversation is applied to a specific performance application. The member first writes what the goal in the conversation is. Next he/she fills in the expanding and focusing phases of the diagram with what he/she would try to achieve during each of these phases.

Time

- 30 minutes.

Materials

- Copy of *Testing Our Understanding of Creating Shape (The Core Conversation)* for each participant (p. 209).

- Overhead, *The Core Conversation* (p. 307).

- Chapter 2, *COACHING: The ASTD Trainer's Sourcebook.*

Directions

1. Review the exercise and its objectives.

2. Assign breakout rooms, if used.

3. Assign time to complete exercise and return to general session.

4. Review the overhead, *The Core Conversation.* Make sure participants make the connection between core conversation and shape. Shape is an essential characteristic. The way we create shape is by using the core conversation. Leave the overhead on screen during the exercise.

Debrief   Field questions.

    Ensure that participants understand shape and relate shape to the core conversation. The core conversation is the shape coaches create through their disciplined behaviors.

<u>HANDOUT</u>   **Testing Our Understanding of Creating Shape (The Core Conversation)**

Time   You have _____ minutes for this exercise.

Objectives   To help participants test their understanding of the definition of creating shape (the core conversation) and to give participants the opportunity to identify communication behaviors that help create shape.

Directions

1. Review this exercise as a team and ensure that your team understands what tasks it must complete.

2. Review as a team the following definition of *creating shape* (the core conversation) and ensure that each member understands the definition.

CREATING SHAPE

The core conversation is the shape that is characteristic of superior coaching conversations. It is the core conversation which is the foundation shape of all superior coaching interactions.

Successful coaching has a recurring shape which is determined by a number of factors. Two of the most important are:

- The goal of the coaching conversation is clearly stated.

- The flow of the conversation first expands information, then focuses the use of the information as the coach and persons being coached move toward the goal.

---

3. Each participant selects one of the following mini cases. Imagine having a coaching conversation using the case. Using the shape of the core conversation, write in under "Performance Applications" what your goal in the conversation is. Be concrete. Next, fill in the expanding and focusing phases of the diagram with what you would try to achieve during each of these phases. Be as concrete as you possibly can.

4. Each person describes his/her coaching conversation to the team. During the presentation, the team should try to help the presenter be as concrete as possible and test his/her understanding of "shaping the coaching conversation."

5. Discuss your experience in this exercise and bring any questions to the general session.

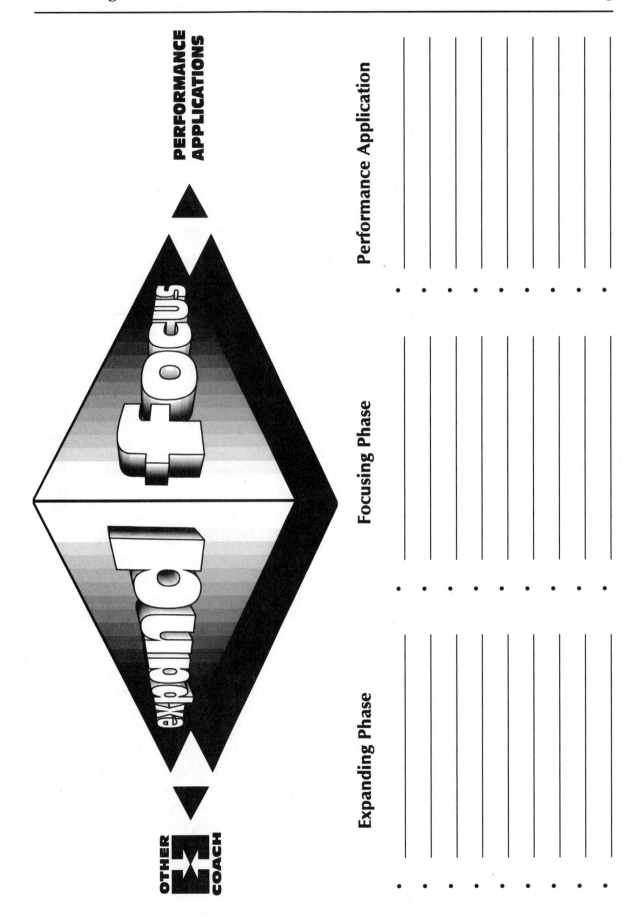

Performance Application

Focusing Phase

Expanding Phase

Mini cases

Case A

> You are teaching a coworker how to edit a paper.

Case B

> An employee has come to you and is complaining about working with another employee.

Case C

> One of your team members demonstrates a great willingness to be an exemplary team member, consistently goes out of his/her way to carry as much of the team's work load as possible, and is immediately responsive to the needs of other team members.

Case D

> You have organized a special team to improve your organization's reward system. Their report is overdue.

Case E

> You have organized your first total quality improvement team and want to help them understand the kinds of improvement opportunities it might address.

Case F

> You have a team developing guidelines to procure personal computer hardware for your organization. You have read the team's progress report and want to give them feedback.

TRAINER'S NOTES   # Testing Our Understanding of Communicating Respect

Objectives   To help participants test their understanding of the definition of respect and give them the opportunity to identify communication behaviors that help create respect and those that do not.

Description   Participants review the definition of communicating respect. They then work as a team and review several mini cases and the alternative statements that a coach might make. They select the statements that they think demonstrate the most respect and indicate why they thought that other statements did not demonstrate respect.

Time   • 30 minutes.

Materials   • Copy of *Testing Our Understanding of Communicating Respect* (p. 213).

• Overhead, *Meaning of Respect* (p. 314).

• Chapter 2, *COACHING: The ASTD Trainer's Sourcebook.*

Directions   1. Review the exercise and its objectives.

2. Assign breakout rooms, if used.

3. Assign time to complete exercise and return to general session.

4. Review the overhead, *Meaning of Respect*. Leave the overhead on screen during the exercise.

Debrief   ☑ Field questions.

☑ Review list of essential characteristics.

☑ Review definition of respect.

Exercise key   Respectful responses:

• Are concrete.

• Focus specifically on the other person's input.

• Are not judgmental.

• Do not criticize.

• Focus on a problem to be solved and not a person to be fixed.

The best responses in this exercise are: A3, B1 or 4, C3, and D2.

<u>HANDOUT</u>	**Testing Our Understanding Of Communicating Respect**
Time	You have _____ minutes for this exercise.
Objectives	To help participants test their understanding of the definition of respect and give them the opportunity to identify communication behaviors that help create respect and those that do not.

Directions

1. Review this exercise as a team and ensure that your team understands what tasks it must complete.

2. Review as a team the following definition of *respect* and ensure that each member understands the definition.

> **Respect**
>
> A qualitative characteristic of successful coaching is that the leader communicates respect for the people being coached. Demonstrating respect is more complicated than avoiding behaviors which communicate that a person is stupid, evil, or inferior. One must also use behaviors in a conversation which involve the other person and make that person a fully accepted player.

3. Work as a team. Read the mini cases and possible responses. Select the one you think demonstrates the most respect. Indicate why you think the others do not demonstrate respect.

4. Bring the results of your team's work from Step 3 to the general session.

Mini Cases

Case A

> You have been trying to teach a coworker how to use a new computer application software. The coworker has been very slow to learn what you are trying to teach.

Coach's Alternative Statements

1. I'm not sure you are ready for this. Either that, or you may not be practicing enough.

2. Try a little harder to keep in mind that the mouse has three buttons and each button has a different function.

3. The help menu can save you a lot of time. The next time you get stuck, I'm not going to give you the answer. Let's see if you can discover the answer yourself.

4. The other people seem to be catching on a bit faster than you are. Do you have any idea why that is?

Case B

> An employee complains to you about feeling dead ended in his/her job.

Coach's Alternative Statements

1. You might find out from other people in the company who have had your experience and ask what they did about it.

2. Careers are funny things. About the best advice I can give is to do superior work and eventually you will get lucky.

3. I don't think anyone is going to be able to give you a cookbook for getting ahead. Each of us is responsible for what happens to us.

4. What specific goals have you got for your self and your career? What jobs have you been working toward?

Case C

> You are giving feedback to a team whose task is to produce criteria for purchasing personal computer equipment. You want to encourage them to stay on schedule. Their outline has created some doubts in your mind that they will get the job done on time.

Coach's Alternative Statements

1. I've read your first report, and the way you have outlined your task makes me doubt that you will ever get the job done.

2. I want to review your report and see how we can eliminate some of the things you plan to do and simplify the task a bit.

3. I've looked at your first report and feel we need to compare your plan with our schedule.

4. We can't count on senior management granting an extension on this project. I think there is a bit of fluff in your plans. Here are some things I think you can omit.

Case D

> You have given an employee several hours of coaching on how to run team meetings. The last one you observed still ran over the allotted time and produced no clear result. You are in a coaching session to help improve the employee's team meeting leadership skills.

Coach's Alternative Statements

1. I noticed you let the meeting get a bit out of hand again. What I am wondering now is if you feel intimidated by your team and are afraid to take charge.

2. Two things happened in your meeting that I observed yesterday. First, you didn't produce a concrete result; second, the meeting ran 15 minutes past the time it was supposed to end. I want to review with you the reasons that I think these things happened.

3. The reason your meeting went a bit off course yesterday was that you failed to review the team's norms at the beginning (like ending on time), and you failed to keep the team on track in its discussions. Someone has got to keep the team conscious and that someone is you. You are the leader.

4. Tell me how you feel about leading your team. You seemed to be so uncertain yesterday about what you were trying to achieve that I begin to think maybe you are pretty insecure in this job.

TRAINER'S NOTES	**Practicing Communicating Respect**

Objectives

To give participants the opportunity to practice behaviors of attending and inquiring and get feedback from their fellow team members.

Description

Each participant imagines that he/she is at the beginning of a coaching conversation for any of the performance applications—resolving problems, teaching new knowledge or skills, supporting performance, and adjusting performance.

They then create some concrete situation in which they are using the performance application that you have selected. They prepare a statement they might use at the beginning or the end of the application that demonstrates respect and a second statement that does not. The team then discusses each statement and gives concrete reasons why members agree that the statement does or does not communicate respect.

Time

• 40 minutes.

Materials

• Copy of *Practicing Communicating Respect* (p. 217).

• Overhead, *Meaning of Respect* (p. 314).

• Chapter 2, *COACHING: The ASTD Trainer's Sourcebook.*

Directions

1. Review the exercise and its objectives.

2. Assign breakout rooms, if used.

3. Assign time to complete exercise and return to general session.

4. Review the overhead, *Meaning of Respect*. Leave the overhead on screen during the exercise.

Debrief

 Have participants give a few examples of their statements that demonstrate respect and those that do not.

 Discuss how the statements differ. The goal is to develop a very concrete and behavioral understanding of respect.

<u>H</u>ANDOUT	**Practicing Communicating Respect**

Time   You have _____ minutes for this exercise.

Objectives   To give participants the opportunity to practice behaviors of attending and inquiring and get feedback from their fellow team members.

Directions

1. Review this exercise as a team and ensure that your team understands what tasks it must complete.

2. Imagine that you are beginning a coaching conversation for any of the following performance applications:

   • Resolving problems.

   • Teaching new knowledge or skills.

   • Supporting performance.

   • Adjusting performance.

3. Create in your mind some concrete situation in which you are using the performance application you have selected.

4. Prepare a statement you might use at the beginning or end of the application you have chosen that demonstrates respect, and a second statement that does not.

5. Each person describes the situation and application that he/she is using, then presents both statements. The team then discusses each statement and gives concrete reasons why members agree that the statement does or does not communicate respect.

6. Discuss your experience in this exercise and bring any questions to the general session.

TRAINER'S NOTES	# Practicing Attending and Inquiring

Objectives

To give participants the opportunity to practice behaviors that communicate attending and inquiring, and get feedback from their fellow team members.

Description

Participants work as teams and review the definition of attending and inquiring. Each team member selects some topic from the list provided to discuss with another team member. Each person uses the topic that he/she has selected and talks to another person. The person being spoken to must demonstrate good attending behavior and use at least one open-ended inquiry and one close-ended inquiry during the interaction. The rest of the team observes and gives feedback.

Time

- 35 minutes.

Materials

- Copy of *Practicing Attending and Inquiring* (p. 219).

- Overhead, *Critical Skills* (p. 315).

- Chapter 2, *COACHING: The ASTD Trainer's Sourcebook.*

Directions

1. Review the exercise and its objectives.

2. Assign breakout rooms, if used.

3. Assign time to complete exercise and return to general session.

4. Review the overhead, *Critical Skills*. Emphasize the definitions of attending and inquiring. Leave the overhead on screen during the exercise.

Debrief   Field questions.

                       Have participants give examples of attending and inquiring.

HANDOUT	**Practicing Attending and Inquiring**

Time

You have _____ minutes for this exercise.

Objectives

To give participants the opportunity to practice behaviors that communicate attending and inquiring, and get feedback from their fellow team members.

Directions

1. Review this exercise as a team and ensure that your team understands what tasks it must complete.

2. Work as a team and review the definition of attending below. Ensure that all team members understand the definition of attending.

ATTENDING

The term attending refers to the vocal and nonvocal techniques used by coaches to convey active listening. Nonvocal behaviors include:

- Facing the other person.

- Keeping comfortable eye contact.

- Nodding in agreement.

- Avoiding distracting behaviors such as fidgeting, thumbing through papers, and interrupting.

The nonvocal aspects of attending encourage the other person to interact easily and to develop the necessary information. Vocal responses such as "Uh huh," "Yes," "I can see that," "OK," etc., communicate to the other person that the coach is paying attention.

In addition, attending behaviors have the effect of disciplining the coach to listen by focusing the coach's concentration on what the other person is saying.

3. Work as a team and review the definition of inquiring. Ensure that all team members understand the definition of inquiring.

INQUIRING

Inquiring takes the following forms:

- **Questions**
  "So what did you do when you learned the contractor was going to be late completing the first phase?"

- **Directives**
  "Tell me what you did when you learned the contractor was going to be late completing the first phase."

Questions and directives may be closed or open. A closed question might be, "Should Jones be included on the team?" An open question might be, "What sort of people do you think we should put on the team?" A closed directive might be, "Tell me how long it will take for you to complete the plan." An open directive might be, "Tell me what you think you must do to complete the plan."

4. Each team member selects a topic from the list below to discuss with another team member:

   • Difficulties you have had with people who have tried to teach you some new skill.

   • How you think your organization could improve its performance.

   • Where you think people in your organization waste the most time.

   • How senior managers have been the least amount of help to you.

   • The most difficult coworker you have ever worked with.

   • What keeps people from listening to you.

5. Seat the team in a circle. Start with any one member. That person uses the topic that he/she has selected from Step 4 and talks to the person to his/her left for one minute. The person being spoken to is responsible for using good attending behavior and for using at least one open-ended inquiry and one close-ended inquiry during the interaction. The rest of the team observes and gives feedback as follows:

   • What nonvocal attending behaviors did the listener use?

   • What vocal attending behaviors did the listener use?

   • How many open ended inquiries were made?

   • How many closed ended inquiries were made?

6. Repeat Step 5 until each person has been observed listening to a fellow team member.

7. Discuss your experience in this exercise and bring any questions to the general session.

<u>TRAINER'S NOTES</u>　　**Practicing Reflecting**

Objectives

To give participants the opportunity to practice behaviors of reflecting and get feedback from their fellow team members.

Description

Participants work as teams and review the definition of reflecting. They then work as individuals and write out a reflecting response to each of a series of statements provided. Team members read their responses and get feedback from their fellow team members.

Time

- 35 minutes.

Materials

- Copy of *Practicing Reflecting* (p. 222).

- Overhead, *Critical Skills* (p. 315).

- Chapter 2, *COACHING: The ASTD Trainer's Sourcebook.*

Directions

1. Review the exercise and its objectives.

2. Assign breakout rooms, if used.

3. Assign time to complete exercise and return to general session.

4. Review the overhead, *Critical Skills*. Give a couple of your own examples of reflecting. Leave the overhead on screen during the exercise. Remind participants that reflecting is one of the skills that is particularly useful during the expanding or information developing phase of a coaching interaction.

Debrief　　Field questions.

　Get examples from participants of reflecting responses to the statements used in the exercise.

<u>H</u>ANDOUT	**Practicing Reflecting**

Time

You have _____ minutes for this exercise.

Objectives

To give participants the opportunity to practice reflecting and get feedback from their fellow team members.

Directions

1. Review this exercise as a team and ensure that your team understands what tasks it must complete.

2. Work as a team and review the definition of reflecting below. Ensure that all team members understand the definition of reflecting.

> ### REFLECTING
>
> Reflecting is not mirroring or repeating verbatim what the other person has said. It is playing back to the other person what the coach believes has been said, and/or communicating the feelings that the other person has conveyed.

Reflecting is illustrated in the following examples:

Other: "It just isn't possible to get the contractor to respond. He has it in his head that he works for his corporate headquarters and not for me."

Coach: "So, you feel almost powerless to get him to do the job you think he should."

Other: "I don't see how I can keep putting my people on all these Total Quality Management (T.Q.M.) teams. I have just enough people to manage our trouble calls. If they are all on teams, it's me that's going to get the flak when somebody has a computer down. My customers don't care about my problems."

Coach: "The way you see it at the moment is that you're in a no-win situation. Management wants you to participate in its T.Q.M. program, but to you that means you may disappoint your customers."

Other: "I don't see how the company can expect me to bust my buns when I know that the more I do, the more I get to do. There is no chance for promotion and our bonus system is a joke."

Coach: "I guess the big issue for you is that you don't feel properly rewarded or valued because of what you do."

3. Work as individuals and write a reflecting response to each of the following statements. Assume that the statements have been made to you.

Statement A

"I don't think there is any way to get ahead in this company. No matter how hard I try, I just get nowhere."

Statement B

"The application we have been told to use just won't do the job. It's too complicated and doesn't produce the kind of graphics we need."

Statement C

"How can we all be expected to work on teams and still be part of our natural work group? I spend more time on T.Q.M. than I do on real work."

Statement D

"It's not that the work is all that complicated. The problem is that the schedule and priorities keep changing. You just don't know from one day to the next what you might be doing."

4. Start with statement A. Have each team member read his/her reflecting response, followed with team feedback. First, indicate if it is a reflecting response—without commenting on its quality. Second, if it is not a reflecting response, help the person reading the response turn it into a reflecting response.

5. Discuss your experience in this exercise and bring any questions to the general session.

<u>Trainer's Notes</u>	# Practicing Attending, Inquiring, and Reflecting

Objectives

To give participants the opportunity to practice behaviors of attending, inquiring, and reflecting, and receive feedback concerning their performance.

Description

Each team member selects a topic from the list provided to discuss with another team member. Arrange the team in a circle. Start with any one member. That person uses the topic that he/she has selected from and talks to the person to his/her left for two minutes. The person being spoken to is responsible for using the attending, inquiring, and reflecting behaviors during the interaction. The rest of the team records its observations on the *Observation Sheet* found on the following page during each interaction. At the end of each interaction, each team member uses the sheet to give feedback to the person being observed.

Time

- 45 minutes.

Materials

- Copy of *Practicing Attending, Inquiring, and Reflecting* for each participant (p. 225).

- Copy of *Observation Sheet* for each observer (p. 226).

- Overhead, *Critical Skills* (p. 315).

- Chapter 2, *COACHING: The ASTD Trainer's Sourcebook.*

Directions

1. Review the exercise and its objectives.

2. Assign breakout rooms, if used.

3. Assign time to complete exercise and return to general session.

4. Review the overhead, *Critical Skills*. Leave the overhead on screen during the exercise.

Debrief

 Field questions.

 Get examples from participants of the three kinds of behavior practiced in the exercise.

<u>H</u>ANDOUT	**Practicing Attending, Inquiring, and Reflecting**
Time	You have _____ minutes for this exercise.
Objectives	To give participants the opportunity to practice behaviors of attending, inquiring, and reflecting, and receive feedback concerning their performance.

Directions

1. Review this exercise as a team and ensure that your team understands what tasks it must complete.

2. Each team member selects a topic from the list below to discuss with another team member:

   - Difficulties you have had with people who have tried to teach you some new skill.

   - How you think your organization could improve its performance.

   - Where you think people in your organization waste the most time.

   - How senior managers have been the least amount of help to you.

   - The most difficult coworker you have ever worked with.

   - What keeps people from listening to you.

3. Arrange the team in a circle. Start with any one member. That person uses the topic that he/she has selected from Step 2 and talks to the person to his/her left for two minutes. The person being spoken to is responsible for using the attending, inquiring, and reflecting behaviors during the interaction. The rest of the team records its observations on the *Observation Sheet*. At the end of each interaction, each team member uses the sheet to give feedback to the person being observed.

4. Discuss your experience in this exercise and bring any questions to the general session.

Observation Sheet

Person Observed	Quality of Nonvocal Attending	Quality of Vocal Attending	Number of Closed Inquiries	Number of Open Inquiries	Number of Reflecting Responses	Remarks

<u>TRAINER'S NOTES</u>   # Practicing Affirmation

Objectives   To give participants the opportunity to practice behaviors that
                       affirm, and receive feedback from their fellow team members.

Description   Participants work as a team and review the definition of affirming.
                       Each team member then selects one of the mini cases provided. Tell
                       members that they are in the process of concluding a coaching ses-
                       sion, using the case selected. Each member writes out a statement
                       that would be appropriate toward the end of such a session that
                       affirms the strengths that other people can be expected to demon-
                       strate on-the-job, and the strengths the person(s) demonstrated dur-
                       ing the coaching session. Members receive feedback on the
                       appropriateness of their affirming statements from their fellow
                       team members.

Time   • 30 minutes.

Materials   • Copy of *Practicing Affirmation* for each participant (p. 228).

                       • Overhead, *Critical Skills* (p. 315).

                       • Chapter 2, *COACHING: The ASTD Trainer's Sourcebook.*

Directions   **1.** Review the exercise and its objectives.

                       2. Assign breakout rooms, if used.

                       3. Assign time to complete exercise and return to general session.

                       4. Review the overhead, *Critical Skills.* Emphasize definition of
                            affirming.

Debrief   Field questions.

                       Get examples from participants of the three kinds of behavior prac-
                                           ticed in the exercise.

<u>H</u>ANDOUT	**Practicing Affirmation**

You have _____ minutes for this exercise.

Objectives   To give participants the opportunity to practice behaviors that affirm, and receive feedback from their fellow team members.

Directions

1. Review this exercise as a team and ensure that your team understands what tasks it must complete.

2. Work as a team and review the definition of affirming found below. Ensure that all team members understand the definition of affirming.

> **AFFIRMING**
>
> Affirming puts into direct action the coach's belief that people want to be competent. Affirming reinforces the sense of competency in the other person and contributes directly to that person's commitment to continuous improvement.
>
> Affirming during a coaching interaction may draw attention to two sets of competencies that the other person has demonstrated: first, those competencies which the person has demonstrated on the job; second, those competencies that the person demonstrates during a coaching interaction.

3. Each team member selects one of the mini cases listed on the next page. Assume that you are in the process of concluding a coaching session, using the case you have selected. Write out a statement that would be appropriate toward the end of such a session that affirms the strengths that other people can be expected to demonstrate on the job, and the strengths the person(s) demonstrated during the coaching session.

Mini Cases

Case A

Your work group is required to submit weekly notes describing major activities, problems, and achievements to senior management. You have been conducting a successful coaching session with an employee who regularly fails to prepare those notes on time.

Case B

You have an employee that never volunteers for tough or dirty jobs, and rarely assists other work group members when they need help. The others' impression is that he/she is willing to do only the minimum amount of work to get by and has little commitment to doing superior work. You are concluding a coaching session to support the employee's performance.

Case C

You just finished a successful coaching session to teach a mature employee how to use the office's new electronic mail system. The person has limited experience with computers.

Case D

You are conducting a coaching session with an employee who is a single parent having a difficult time caring for his/her children and staying on the company's work hour schedule.

4. Each person describes, in turn, the case that he/she is using, then gives the affirming statement that he/she has written in Step 3. The team then discusses each statement and gives concrete reasons why members agree that the statement does or does not affirm.

5. Discuss your experience in this exercise and bring any questions to the general session.

Notes

- _____
- _____
- _____
- _____
- _____
- _____
- _____
- _____
- _____
- _____
- _____
- _____
- _____
- _____
- _____
- _____
- _____
- _____
- _____
- _____
- _____
- _____
- _____

Resolving Problems

PRACTICE INTERACTION—PERFORMANCE APPLICATION

Objectives

To give participants the opportunity to practice all the elements in the Superior Coaching Model and apply these elements to a performance application that focuses on resolving problems. Participants are given feedback on the demonstrated competency in using the Superior Coaching Model and using it in the performance application, *Resolving Problems*.

Description

Members work in teams. Breakout rooms are required. In this exercise each member takes a turn at serving as a coach and practices using the performance application, *Resolving Problems*. Interactions should be videotaped, if possible. Each member receives feedback on how well he/she used the elements in the Superior Coaching Model in carrying out the coaching conversation.

Time

- 2 hours.

Materials

- Copy of *Resolving Problems*.
  (Practice Interaction—Performance Application) (p. 232).

- Copy of *Observation Sheet* (for each participant) (p. 237).

- Breakout rooms.

- Videotaping and replay equipment for each team—if possible.

- Overhead, *The Four Performance Applications* (p. 308).

- Overhead, *Resolving Problems Performance Application*
  (p. 316).

Directions

1. Review the exercise and its objectives.

2. Assign breakout rooms.

3. Assign time to complete exercise and return to general session.

4. Review the overheads, *The Four Performance Applications* and *Resolving Problems Performance Application*. Ensure definition of resolving problems is clear.

Debrief Collect and discuss the participants' key learnings.

<u>H</u>ANDOUT	## Resolving Problems

PRACTICE INTERACTION—PERFORMANCE APPLICATION

Time

You have _____ minutes for this exercise.

Objectives

To give participants the opportunity to practice all the elements in the Superior Coaching Model and apply the elements to a performance application that focuses on resolving problems. Participants are given feedback on the demonstrated competency in using the Superior Coaching Model and using it in the performance application, *Resolving Problems*.

Directions

1. Review the sequence of this exercise and all the tasks as a team and ensure that your team understands how the exercise is conducted.

   Each person will serve the two functions of "Other" and "Coach." However, these are not "roles." You are at all times yourselves. The purpose of the exercise is to practice skills. The scenario that you will use provides you with content for practicing the Superior Coaching Model and its skills. You are not trying to play a part that is foreign to yourself.

   Other: Your job in this exercise is to give the coach an opportunity to practice. Do not be overly obtuse or difficult.

   Coach: When you are in this function in the exercise, your primary objective is to practice your understanding of the Superior Coaching Model, i.e., demonstrate your values of coaching, creating the essential characteristics, and using the critical skills to create the core conversation. Go as far as you can in the conversation.

2. Review as a team the following definition of the *Resolving Problems* application of coaching to ensure that everyone understands it.

> ### RESOLVING PROBLEMS
>
> The performance application of coaching includes the many kinds of conversations in which managers and leaders work to resolve a wide variety of problems presented to them by others. The problems may be technical; they may relate to schedules or organizational relationships; they may pertain to careers; they may be personal. When you use the core conversation to chart what should be happening in a conversation to resolve problems, look for specific events in each of the two phases.

3. Prepare for the practice coaching session by assigning each member of your team a letter.

Letter	Team Member
A	
B	
C	
D	
E	
F	
G	

4. Review the appropriate exercise sequence and make sure the team knows how to proceed. During each interaction, the person serving as the timer will:

- Run the video (if used).

- Keep time and limit the practice session to five minutes for each coach.

All other members of the team who are not serving as timer, coach, or person being coached, are observers. Their job is to:

- Observe the performance of the coach.

- Complete the *Observation Sheet* on the person serving as coach.

- Use the *Observation Sheet* and give feedback to the person practicing as coach.

Exercise sequence with video:

a. Conduct and tape practice interaction (5 minutes).

b. Discuss and give feedback (___ minutes).

c. Replay tape and critique (___ minutes).

d. Repeat Steps 1 to 4 until each member has served as coach.

Exercise sequence without video:

a. Conduct practice interaction (5 minutes).

b. Discuss and give feedback (___ minutes).

c. Repeat Steps 1, 2, and 4 until each member has served as coach.

Expanding phase

In the *expanding* phase of a problem solving interaction, the coach will develop information that leads to a mutual understanding of the:

- Problem or problems.
- History of the problem.
- Cause(s) of the problem.
- Implications if the problem is not resolved.

Focusing phase

In the *focusing* phase of a problem solving interaction, the coach will use the information developed in the expanding phase to mutually:

- Develop alternative strategies for resolving the problem.
- Agree on a plan to resolve the problem.
- Agree on a follow-up plan to track progress.

In this exercise each member of your team will take a turn at serving as a coach and responding to a problem presented by one other team member. However, to function as the person with the problem, you must first have one. Select from the list on the next page the problem that you will present to your coach during the practice session.

Notes

- _____
- _____
- _____
- _____
- _____
- _____
- _____
- _____
- _____
- _____
- _____
- _____
- _____
- _____
- _____
- _____
- _____

Problem A

You are a conscientious employee who is a single parent. Your two children, ages 10 and 12, live with you. You serve on a computer repair team that is on call during the regular working day. Members of the team take turns being on call during the weekends and after hours. You are having trouble working the 9 to 5 day and taking your regular turn on call because of your many parental responsibilities. You meet with your supervisor to try to resolve the problem.

Problem B

You don't like working on teams. You have always worked independently as a budget analyst. Now you have been put on several teams to improve various fiscal systems. You don't want to work on teams and meet with your supervisor to resolve the problem.

Problem C

You work on a team of mechanics which repairs the company's heating and air conditioning equipment. You are new to the team and feel the older members are unwilling to give you any serious work to do. You feel that you are a "go for." You meet with the person who supervises several such teams to resolve the problem.

Problem D

You had some health problems during the last performance appraisal period and missed a good bit of work. You have recently received a performance appraisal from your supervisor that is lower than what you think you deserved. Your supervisor has been unwilling to change your appraisal and give you a higher rating. You meet with your supervisor's manager to resolve the problem.

Problem E

You are an engineer who shares one secretary with four other engineers in your section. You feel that the secretary doesn't like you and gives the other engineers preferential treatment with their reports. You have confronted the secretary with the issue, but have not been able to get the response you think you merit. You meet with your team leader to resolve the problem.

Problem F

You feel the company is not doing enough to support the careers of women and/or certain ethnic groups. Your concern is that so few from these groups are in middle management positions, and none are in senior management positions. You have not been promoted as fast as you feel your performance merits and are afraid your own career is going to suffer. You meet with a representative from personnel to resolve your problem.

Problem G

You work in a group responsible for selecting the computer software and hardware to automate a state's library system. One problem that has surfaced several times is that your manager purchases software and hardware without consulting the engineers and technicians in your group. You are the administrative assistant to the manager and can see the waste resulting from the manager's behavior. You meet with one of the consultants that the group has used in order to search for ways to help resolve the problem and still keep your job.

Observation Sheet

1. Did the coach create the following characteristics?

Characteristic	Examples of Specific Behaviors That Helped Create Characteristic	Comments
Balance		
Concreteness		
Shared Responsibility		
Shape		
Respect		

2. How often and/or how well did the coach use the following skills?

Skill	Frequency (For attending note quality)	Comments
Attending		
Closed Inquiries		
Open Inquiries		
Reflecting		
Affirming		

3. How well did the coach accomplish the following in the expanding phase of the conversation?

- Mutual understanding of the problem.

- Mutual understanding of the history of the problem.

- Mutual understanding of the causes of the problem.

- Mutual understanding of the implications, if problem not resolved.

4. How well did the coach accomplish the following in the focusing phase of the conversation?

- Mutual understanding of the history of the problem.

- Mutual understanding of the causes of the problem.

- Mutual understanding of the implications, if problem not resolved.

TRAINER'S NOTES	# Teaching

PRACTICE INTERACTION—PERFORMANCE APPLICATION

Objectives

To give participants the opportunity to practice all the elements in the Superior Coaching Model and apply all these elements to a performance application that focuses on teaching. Participants are given feedback on their demonstrated competency in using the Superior Coaching Model and using it in the performance application, *Teaching*.

Description

Members work in teams. Breakout rooms are required. In this exercise each member takes a turn at serving as a coach and practices using the performance application, *Teaching*. Interactions should be videotaped, if at all possible. Each member receives feedback on how well he/she used the elements in the Superior Coaching Model in carrying out the coaching conversation.

Time

• 2 hours.

Materials

• Copy of *Teaching* (Practice Interaction—Performance Application) for each participant (p. 239).

• Copy of *Observation Sheet* (for each participant) (p. 243).

• Overhead, *The Four Performance Applications* (p. 308).

• Overhead, *Teaching Performance Application* (p. 318).

• Breakout rooms.

• Videotaping and replay equipment for each team—if at all possible.

Directions

1. Review the exercise and its objectives.

2. Assign breakout rooms.

3. Assign time to complete exercise and return to general session.

4. Review the overheads, *The Four Performance Applications* and *Teaching Performance Application*. Ensure definition of teaching is clear.

Debrief Collect and discuss the participants' key learnings.

HANDOUT

Teaching

PRACTICE INTERACTION—PERFORMANCE APPLICATION

Time

You have _____ minutes for this exercise.

Objectives

To give participants the opportunity to practice all the elements in the Superior Coaching Model and apply all these elements to a performance application that focuses on teaching. Participants are given feedback on the demonstrated competency in using the Superior Coaching Model and using it in the performance application, *Teaching*.

Directions

1. Review the sequence of this exercise and all the tasks as a team and ensure that your team understands how the exercise is conducted.

Each person will serve the two functions of "Other" and "Coach." However, these are not "roles." You are at all times yourselves. The purpose of the exercise is to practice skills. The scenario that you will use provides you with content for practicing the Superior Coaching Model and its skills. You are not trying to play a part that is foreign to yourself.

Other: Your job in this exercise is to give the coach an opportunity to practice. Do not be overly obtuse or difficult.

Coach: When you are in this function in the exercise, your primary objective is to practice your understanding of the Superior Coaching Model, i.e., demonstrate your values of coaching, create the essential characteristics, and use the critical skills to create the core conversation. Go as far as you can in the conversation.

2. Review as a team the following definition of the *Teaching* application of coaching and ensure that everyone understands what this application is and that this is the application you are practicing in this exercise.

> ### TEACHING
>
> One primary function of coaches is that they teach. Coaches use personal interactions to increase the competencies of individuals and teams. When we apply the core conversation to teaching, we can see what the superior coach is conscious of trying to achieve in each phase of the conversation.

Expanding phase

In the expanding phase of a teaching interaction the coach will develop information that leads to a mutual understanding of:

- What the coach wants the other person to learn, i.e., the goals of the conversation.

- What the other person already knows.

- How the conversation will proceed, i.e., the sequence.

Focusing phase

In the focusing phase of the interaction the coach will use the information developed in the expanding phase to:

- Teach the content that the other person needs to learn.

- Request feedback or a demonstration to ensure that learning has occurred.

- Clear up any residual questions the other person might have.

3. In this exercise each member of your team will take a turn at coaching the rest of the team. Assign one of the topics listed below to each team member:

   - How to improve team communication.

   - How to evaluate team performance.

   - How to use all the team's resources.

   - How to get more out of the program exercises.

   - How to make better use of the team's time.

   - How team members can transfer their learning from the program to their jobs.

   - How team members can continue to practice the skills they have learned at the program.

   - How to use the Superior Coaching Model to continue to improve one's coaching skills.

4. Prepare for the practice coaching session by assigning each member of your team a letter.

Letter	Team Member
A	
B	
C	
D	
E	
F	
G	

5. Review the information that follows and make sure the team knows how to proceed. During each interaction the observer/ timer does the following:

- Runs the video.

- Completes the *Observation Sheet* on the person serving as coach.

- Keeps time and limits the practice session to 5 minutes for each coach.

- At the end of the session, uses the *Observation Sheet* and gives feedback to the person practicing as coach.

Exercise sequence with video:

a. Tape practice interaction between members A and B; observers record observations.

b. Discuss interaction and provide feedback to person functioning as the coach.

c. Replay tape after each interaction and discuss.

d. Repeat sequence outlined in Steps 1 to 3 until each member has served as coach.

Exercise sequence without video:

a. Members A and B practice interaction; observers record observations.

b. Discuss interaction and provide feedback to person functioning as the coach.

c. Repeat Steps 1 and 2 until each member has served as coach.

6. Use the following practice schedule to conduct the practice coaching sessions.

Practice Schedule

Coach	Other	Timer/Observers
A	B	C,D,E,F,G*
B	C	D,E,F,G,A*
C	D	E,F,G,A,B*
D	E	F,G,A,B,C*
E	F	G,A,B,C,D*
F	G	A,B,C,D,E*
G	A	B,C,D,E,F*
		(*Timer)

7. After everyone has served as a coach and received feedback, discuss the exercise as a team and identify three key learning points—what did you learn from doing the exercise? What would you like to remember to help you do a better job coaching others to use a new competency? Bring your key learning points to the general session.

Giving feedback

Remember, to give useful feedback you must:

- Be specific and concrete.

- Be descriptive about behavior (what you see and hear).

- Be free of opinion and interpretation.

- Offer practical recommendations for improvement.

Notes

- _____

- _____

- _____

- _____

- _____

- _____

- _____

- _____

- _____

- _____

- _____

Observation Sheet

Each designated observer in this exercise will use this observation sheet to record the person's behavior who is practicing coaching skills and then use the sheet to give feedback.

1. Did the coach create the following characteristics?

Characteristic	Examples of Specific Behaviors That Helped Create Characteristic	Comments
Balance		
Concreteness		
Shared Responsibility		
Shape		
Respect		

2. How often and/or how well did the coach use the following skills?

Skill	Frequency (For attending note quality)	Comments
Attending		
Closed Inquiries		
Open Inquiries		
Reflecting		
Affirming		

3. How well did the coach accomplish the following in the expanding phase of the conversation?

   • Mutual understanding of what the coach wanted the other person(s) to learn.

   • Mutual understanding of what the other person(s) already know.

   • Mutual understanding of how the conversation will proceed, i.e., what is the sequence, what will happen first, second, and so forth.

4. How well did the coach accomplish the following in the focusing phase of the conversation?

   • Teach the content that the other person needs to learn.

   • Check to ensure (by feedback or demonstration) that learning has occurred.

   • Clear up any residual questions that the other person(s) had.

TRAINER'S NOTES	# Supporting Performance

PRACTICE INTERACTION—PERFORMANCE APPLICATION

Objectives
To give participants the opportunity to practice all the elements in the Superior Coaching Model and apply all these elements to a performance application that focuses on supporting performance. Participants are given feedback on the demonstrated competency in using the Superior Coaching Model and using it in the performance application, *Supporting Performance.*

Description
Members work in teams. Breakout rooms are required. In this exercise each member takes a turn at serving as a coach and practices using the performance application, *Supporting Performance.* Interactions should be videotaped, if at all possible. Each member receives feedback on how well he/she used the elements in the Superior Coaching Model in carrying out the coaching conversation.

Time
- 2 hours.

Materials
- Copy of *Supporting Performance* (Practice Interaction—Performance Application) (p. 245).

- Copy of *Observation Sheet* (for each participant) (p. 251).

- Overhead, *The Four Performance Applications* (p. 308).

- Overhead, *Supporting Performance Application* (p. 320).

- Breakout rooms.

- Replay equipment for each team—if at all possible.

Directions
1. Review the exercise and its objectives.

2. Assign breakout rooms.

3. Assign time to complete exercise and return to general session.

4. Review the overheads, *The Four Performance Applications* and *Supporting Performance Application.*

5. Ensure definition of supporting performance is clear.

Debrief ☑ Collect and discuss the participants' key learnings.

<u>H</u>ANDOUT   **Supporting Performance**

PRACTICE INTERACTION—PERFORMANCE APPLICATION

Time   You have _____ minutes for this exercise.

Objectives   To give participants the opportunity to practice all the elements in
                    the Superior Coaching Model and apply all these elements to a per-
                    formance application that focuses on supporting performance. Par-
                    ticipants are given feedback on the demonstrated competency in
                    using the Superior Coaching Model and using it in the performance
                    application, *Supporting Performance*.

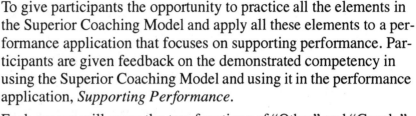

Each person will serve the two functions of "Other" and "Coach."
However, these are not "roles." You are at all times yourselves. The
purpose of the exercise is to practice skills. The scenario that you
will use provides you with content for practicing the Superior
Coaching Model and its skills. You are not trying to play a part that
is foreign to yourself.

Other: Your job in this exercise is to give the coach an opportu-
              nity to practice. Do not be overly obtuse or difficult.

Coach: When you are in this function in the exercise, your pri-
              mary objective is to practice your understanding of the
              Superior Coaching Model, i.e., demonstrate your values
              of coaching, creating the essential characteristics, and
              using the critical skills to create the core conversation.
              Go as far as you can in the conversation.

Directions   1. Review the sequence of this exercise and all the tasks as a team
                        and ensure that your team understands how the exercise is
                        conducted.

                        Exercise sequence with video:

                        a. Tape practice interaction between members A and B;
                            observers record observations.
                        b. Discuss interaction and provide feedback to person
                            functioning as the coach.
                        c. Replay tape after each interaction and discuss.
                        d. Repeat sequence outlined in Steps 1 to 3 until each member
                            has served as coach.

                        Exercise sequence without video:

                        a. Members A and B practice interaction; observers record
                            observations.
                        b. Discuss interaction and provide feedback to person
                            functioning as the coach.
                        c. Repeat Steps 1 and 2 until each member has served as
                            coach.

2. Review as a team the following definition of the *Supporting Performance* application of coaching and ensure that everyone understands what this application is and that this is the application you are practicing in this exercise.

SUPPORTING PERFORMANCE

In addition to teaching and resolving problems presented by others, coaches also interact with individuals and teams to support their performance. Supporting performance can mean giving information about changes in requirements or expectations, or giving feedback to assure others that their performance is on target, or expressing appreciation for the performance of others.

In the expanding phase of a coaching interaction to support performance the coach will develop this sort of information:

*   Clear description of performance being discussed.

*   Clarification of expectations concerning the performance.

*   Mutual understanding of importance of the performance.

In the focusing phase of this interaction the coach will use the information developed in the expanding phase to accomplish such things as:

*   Giving feedback about the performance.

*   Mutual agreement about changes in performance requirements or expectations.

*   Expressing appreciation for performance.

3. In this exercise each member of your team will take a turn at coaching the team using the application *Supporting Performance*. Select from the list a mini case that you will use when you serve as coach and practice supporting performance. Feel free to modify the case to meet your own needs. More than one person may use the same case.

Mini cases   **Case A**

> Your team has been involved in designing a new management education system for the company for the past twelve months. Senior management has decided to delay changing the current system. This could mean that a lot of work will never be used and the team may not stay together to finish the project. You have called the team together to break the news about the change and keep it committed to superior performance.

Case B

> Your team has finished its work to give the company guidelines for purchasing personal computers and software. Senior management is in disagreement about the report and may not accept it. You have met with the team to break the news and express appreciation for the team's work.

Case C

> You are holding your regular Friday afternoon meeting with your work team. Your team is responsible for maintenance trouble calls. The team recently was told by senior management that it would be reduced in size and still take over responsibility for a large new building originally designated for outside contract maintenance. You have called a team meeting.

Case D

> Your team is in the business of printing and reproduction. It is in the process of changing over to some new presses and has not been able to keep up with its work load schedule. Many complaints are coming in (all in your mind unreasonable and unfounded). You have called a team meeting.

Case E

> Your team is responsible for the company's total quality management and continuous improvement initiative. It has made some significant achievements, but you would like to help the team focus more on gaining the full support of middle management and first line supervisors. You are meeting with the team to give it feedback on its success and to get it to commit to the new focus.

Case F

> Your team has received the results of an organizational survey which indicates that it rates lower than other teams on its commitment to doing superior work. The team has an excellent work record. You want to make sure that it uses the information it has received from the survey in a positive way. You have called the team together to affirm its achievements and to help it use the survey data in a useful way.

Notes

- _____
- _____
- _____
- _____
- _____
- _____
- _____
- _____
- _____
- _____
- _____
- _____
- _____
- _____
- _____
- _____
- _____

4. Prepare for the practice coaching session by assigning each member of your team (the people at your table) a letter.

Letter	Team Member
A	
B	
C	
D	
E	
F	
G	

5. Review the information that follows and make sure the team knows how to proceed. During each interaction the observer/timer does the following:

- Runs the video.

- Completes the *Observation Sheet* on the person serving as coach.

- Keeps time and limits the practice session to 5 minutes for each coach.

- At the end of the practice coaching session, uses the *Observation Sheet* and gives feedback to the person practicing as coach.

Notes

- _____
- _____
- _____
- _____
- _____
- _____
- _____
- _____
- _____
- _____
- _____

6. Use the practice schedule found below and conduct the practice coaching sessions.

Coach	Other
A	B
B	C
C	D
D	E
E	F
F	G
G	A

7. After everyone has served as a coach and received feedback, discuss the exercise as a team and identify three key learning points—what did you learn from doing the exercise? What would you like to remember to help you do a better job coaching others to support their performance? Bring your key learning points to the general session.

Notes

- _____
- _____
- _____
- _____
- _____
- _____
- _____
- _____
- _____
- _____
- _____
- _____
- _____
- _____
- _____
- _____
- _____

Observation Sheet

1. Did the coach create the following characteristics?

Characteristic	Examples of Specific Behaviors That Helped Create Characteristic	Comments
Balance		
Concreteness		
Shared Responsibility		
Shape		
Respect		

2. How well did the coach accomplish the following in the expanding phase of the conversation?

- Clear description of performance being discussed.

- Clarification of expectations concerning the performance.

- Mutual understanding of importance of the performance.

3. How often and/or how well did the coach use the following skills?

Skill	Frequency (For attending note quality)	Comments
Attending		
Closed Enquiries		
Open Enquiries		
Reflecting		
Affirming		

4. How well did the coach accomplish the following in the focusing phase of the conversation?

- Giving feedback about the performance.

- Mutual agreement about changes in performance requirements or expectations.

- Expressing appreciation for performance.

<u>Trainer's Notes</u>	## Adjusting Performance

Practice Interaction—Performance Application

Objectives
To give participants the opportunity to practice all the elements in the Superior Coaching Model and apply all these elements to a performance application that focuses on adjusting performance. Participants are given feedback on the demonstrated competency in using the Superior Coaching Model and using it in the performance application, *Adjusting Performance*.

Description
Members work in teams. Breakout rooms are required. In this exercise each member takes a turn at serving as a coach and practices using the performance application, *Adjusting Performance*. Interactions should be video taped, if at all possible. Each member receives feedback on how well he/she used the elements in the Superior Coaching Model in carrying out the coaching conversation.

Time
• 2 hours.

Materials
• Copy of *Adjusting Performance*
(Practice Interaction—Performance Application) (p. 254).

• Overhead, *The Four Performance Applications* (p. 308).

• Overhead, *Adjusting Performance Application* (p. 322).

• Breakout rooms.

• Replay equipment for each team—if at all possible.

Directions
1. Review the exercise and its objectives.

2. Assign breakout rooms.

3. Assign time to complete exercise and return to general session.

4. Review the overhead, *Adjusting Performance Application*. Ensure definition of adjusting performance is clear.

Debrief   Collect and discuss the participants' key learnings.

Exercise sequence with video:

a. Tape practice interaction between members A and B; observers record observations.

b. Discuss interaction and provide feedback to person functioning as the coach.

c. Replay tape after each interaction and discuss.

d. Repeat sequence outlined in Steps 1 to 3 until each member has served in function of coach.

Exercise sequence without video:

a. Members A and B practice interaction; observers record observations.

b. Discuss interaction and provide feedback to person functioning as the coach.

c. Repeat Steps 1 and 2 until each member has served in function of coach.

Notes

- _____
- _____
- _____
- _____
- _____
- _____
- _____
- _____
- _____
- _____
- _____
- _____
- _____
- _____
- _____
- _____
- _____
- _____

<u>HANDOUT</u>	**Adjusting Performance**

PRACTICE INTERACTION—PERFORMANCE APPLICATION

Time

You have _____ minutes for this exercise.

Objectives

To give participants the opportunity to practice all the elements in the Superior Coaching Model and apply all these elements to a performance application that focuses on adjusting performance. Participants are given feedback on the demonstrated competency in using the Superior Coaching Model and using it in the performance application, *Adjusting Performance*.

Each person will serve the two functions of "Other" and "Coach." However, these are not "roles." You are at all times yourselves. The purpose of the exercise is to practice skills. The scenario that you will use provides you with content for practicing the Superior Coaching Model and its skills. You are not trying to play a part that is foreign to yourself.

Other: Your job in this exercise is to give the coach an opportunity to practice. Do not be overly obtuse or difficult.

Coach: When you are in this function in the exercise, your primary objective is to practice your understanding of the Superior Coaching Model, i.e., demonstrate your values of coaching, creating the essential characteristics, and using the critical skills to create the core conversation. Go as far as you can in the conversation.

Directions

1. Review the sequence of this exercise and all the tasks as a team and ensure that your team understands how the exercise is conducted.

2. Review as a team the definition of the *Adjusting Performance* application to ensure that everyone understands what this application is and that this is the application you are practicing in this exercise.

3. In this exercise each member of your team will take a turn at serving as a coach and adjusting the performance represented by one other team member. To function as the coach you will use one of the mini cases that follows. Select the mini case that you will use when you practice adjusting performance.

4. Prepare for the practice coaching session by assigning each member of your team (the people at your table) a letter.

Letter	Team Member
A	
B	
C	
D	
E	
F	
G	

5. Review the information that follows and make sure the team knows how to proceed. During each interaction, the timer/observer does the following:

- Runs the video (if used).

- Keeps time and limits the practice session to 5 minutes for each coach.

- Completes the *Observation Sheet* on the person serving as coach.

- At the end of the practice coaching session, uses the *Observation Sheet* and gives feedback to the person practicing as coach.

Exercise sequence with video:

a. Tape practice interaction between members A and B; observers record observations.

b. Discuss interaction and provide feedback to person functioning as the coach.

c. Replay tape after each interaction and discuss.

d. Repeat sequence outlined in Steps 1 to 3 until each member has served as coach.

Exercise sequence without video:

a. Members A and B practice interaction; observers record observations.

b. Discuss interaction and provide feedback to person functioning as the coach.

c. Repeat Steps 1 and 2 until each member has served as coach.

6. Use the following practice schedule and conduct the practice coaching sessions.

Coach	Other	Timer/Observers
A	B	C,D,E,F,G*
B	C	D,E,F,G,A*
C	D	E,F,G,A,B*
D	E	F,G,A,B,C*
E	F	G,A,B,C,D*
F	G	A,B,C,D,E*
G	A	B,C,D,E,F*
		(*Timer)

7. After everyone has served as a coach and received feedback, discuss the exercise as a team and identify three key learning points—what did you learn from the exercise? What would you like to remember to help you do a better job coaching others to improve performance? Bring your key learning points to the general session.

Giving feedback

Remember, to give useful feedback you must:

- Be specific and concrete.

- Be descriptive about behavior (what you see and hear).

- Be free of opinion and interpretation.

- Offer practical recommendations for improvement.

Notes

- _____

- _____

- _____

- _____

- _____

- _____

- _____

- _____

- _____

- _____

- _____

Definition of Adjusting
Performance Application of Coaching

Coaches not only teach, resolve problems, and support performance, at times, they must make significant adjustments in the performance of individuals and teams. They must confront performance that is below expectations or established standards, and they must challenge people who are performing at one level to move to a higher level, i.e., people who should be taking on more difficult tasks and assignments.

When we apply the core conversation to adjusting performance, we can expect the following kinds of things to be achieved in each phase.

In the expanding phase of a coaching interaction to adjust performance the coach will develop this sort of information:

- Specific performance being discussed.

- Concrete statement of what the coach believes to be the problem in performance.

- The other person's understanding of the problem.

- Agreement concerning the nature of the performance problem.

- Clarity about who is responsible for resolving the problem.

- Alternative strategies for resolving the problem.

In the focusing phase of this interaction the coach will use the information developed in the expanding phase to accomplish such things as:

- Agreement on what performance will be adjusted and to what degree.

- Agreement on plan to adjust performance.

- Agreement on a follow-up plan to monitor progress.

Mini cases

Case A

Your work group is required to submit weekly notes to senior management. You have an employee who regularly fails to prepare his/her weekly notes on time describing major activities, problems, and achievements.

Case B

You have an employee that never volunteers for tough or dirty jobs. The employee rarely assists other work group members when they need help. The general impression that the employee makes is that he/she is willing only to do the minimum amount of work to get by and has little commitment to doing superior work. You recently asked the employee to stay late one evening to help the team rearrange the office and the employee refused. You have called the employee in to adjust his/her performance.

Case C

You have been assigned along with another coworker the task of looking at ways to improve career planning for employees. You have been unsuccessful in getting your coworker to schedule meetings with you and take his/her fair share of the work. You have gone to see the coworker to adjust his/her performance.

Case D

You have a new supervisor recently promoted by you. The supervisor is responsible for an office automation project, and has begun to fall behind in some of the milestones. You have discussed this problem with the supervisor previously. You noted improvement for a while, but the project has again begun to fall behind schedule.

Case E

Your secretary has become lax about ensuring that your telephone is answered promptly and courteously. He/she sometimes leaves the office without notifying you or arranging for another person to answer the phone. You have just been called to task by your boss because your boss was unable to reach you by phone this morning while you were at a meeting.

Case F

You are angry at a peer who criticized your department in the presence of your boss. You feel the criticism was uncalled for and was in poor taste. You feel that the criticism reflects on you personally and that, at the least, your associate could have made the criticism to you in private. You have arranged a meeting with your associate to repair the damage and insure that your associate doesn't repeat this sort of behavior again.

Case G

You feel strongly that you are not getting enough information from your boss about changes in production schedules which impact on your work group. Your group fabricates metal custom products designed by engineering. Engineers have been coming to your shop asking for products that your boss promised on schedules without discussing the schedules with you or your team.

Case H

You have an employee who has demonstrated great competence as a drafter. You feel the person is wasting his/her talents and want to challenge the employee to go back to school and become qualified as an engineer.

Observation Sheet

1. Did the coach create the following characteristics?

Characteristic	Examples of Specific Behaviors That Helped Create Characteristic	Comments
Balance		
Concreteness		
Shared Responsibility		
Shape		
Respect		

2. How often and/or how well did the coach use the following skills?

Skill	Frequency (For attending note quality)	Comments
Attending		
Closed Inquiries		
Open Inquiries		
Reflecting		
Affirming		

3. How well did the coach accomplish the following in the expanding phase of the conversation?

   • Specify performance being discussed.

   • Concrete statement of what the coach believes to be the problem in performance.

   • The other person's understanding of the problem.

   • Agreement concerning the nature of the performance problem.

   • Clarity about who is responsible for resolving the problem.

   • Alternative strategies for resolving the problem.

4. How well did the coach accomplish the following in the focusing phase of the conversation?

   • Agreement on what performance will be adjusted and to what degree.

   • Agreement on plan to adjust performance.

   • Agreement on a follow-up plan to monitor progress.

Learning Transfer Tools

The materials in this section have been designed to ensure that participants:

- Stay actively involved in their own learning process.

- Assume responsibility for their learning.

- Organize their learning during the coaching skills programs.

- Reinforce their learning during the coaching skills programs.

- Continue to reinforce their learning after the programs end.

- Apply what they learned to their jobs and work environments.

The transfer of learning is one of the more difficult problems facing providers of training and development programs.

- The short term goal of all training is that participants obtain new knowledge or skills.

- The intermediate goal is the application of that knowledge and skills to their jobs.

- The long term goal is that, by using their new knowledge and skills, they make a positive difference in the performance of their organizations.

The materials in this section do not assess learning. The tools for assessing learning are such things as pre and post tests, anecdotes from participants, and feedback from the coworkers of participants. Using tools to assess learning can certainly be used in conjunction with tools to ensure the transfer of learning.

Tools to transfer learning fall into two general categories:

- Tools the individual can use without involving others.

- Tools requiring individuals to work with others.

Whenever possible both sorts of tools should be employed as supplements and reinforcements to each other.

The one-, two-, and three-day designs in Chapters 6, 7, and 8 use at least one tool to transfer and reinforce learning. When you plan your program, make copies of the materials from this chapter that you need.

Review and Action Log

Objectives

The purpose of the R&A log is to help participants record:

- What they learn.

- How they can apply or reinforce the learning.

Materials

- Handout, *Review and Action Log* (p. 263).

Directions

Use the R&A logs as:

- Individual learning tools.

- Sources for discussion and amplification by participants in their review and action teams.

Notes

- _____
- _____
- _____
- _____
- _____
- _____
- _____
- _____
- _____
- _____
- _____
- _____
- _____
- _____
- _____
- _____
- _____
- _____
- _____
- _____
- _____
- _____

HANDOUT   Review and Action Log

Work by yourself and complete this log each time you are requested to do so by your facilitator. You will also review your logs with your assigned review and action team during the program.

Key Learning Points	How I Can Apply or Reinforce What I Have Learned

TRAINER'S NOTES	# Review and Action Teams

Objectives To reinforce and apply learning.

Materials
- Handout, *Review and Action Teams* (p. 265).

Directions Participants in the two- and three-day programs are assigned to a review and action team (R&A team) and stay with that team throughout the program.

Teams

- Meet at specified times to review their experience in the program, key learning points, and discuss their personal action plans.
- Use their R&A logs in these meetings.

Organizations

If participants are attending the program with others from their organization, they are expected to:

- Meet periodically with their R&A team members to continue reinforcing and applying what they learned during the program.

Individuals

If participants are not attending the program with people from their own organization, they are expected to:

- Work with at least one other person in their own organization (a "buddy") to help them continue to reinforce and apply what they learned during the program.

Notes
- _____
- _____
- _____
- _____
- _____
- _____
- _____
- _____
- _____
- _____

<u>HANDOUT</u>   **Review and Action Teams**

1. Write the name, organization and phone number of your R&A team members:

Name	Organization	Phone Number

2. If you are attending the program with others from your organization, meet periodically with your R&A team members to continue reinforcing and applying what you learned during the program:

Date of Next Meeting	Location	Phone Number

3. If you are not attending the program with people from your organization, upon your return, identify at least one other person (a "buddy") to help you continue to reinforce and apply what you learned during the program:

Buddy Name	Phone Number

TRAINER'S NOTES

Buddy System

Objectives

To reinforce and apply learning.

Materials

- Handout, *Buddy System* (p. 267).

Directions

When it is not possible for participants to meet with an R&A team to follow up their experience in the program, it is recommended that they identify one other person with whom to meet. If two persons are present from the same organization in the program, they are logical candidates.

Notes

- _____
- _____
- _____
- _____
- _____
- _____
- _____
- _____
- _____
- _____
- _____
- _____
- _____
- _____
- _____
- _____
- _____
- _____
- _____
- _____

HANDOUT   Buddy System

Directions

One way for you to reinforce and transfer your experience from this program is to identify a person with whom you will meet after the program for at least three sessions to discuss what you learned in the program, and what you are doing to improve your coaching skills. Complete this planning sheet before you leave the program:

Name:	
Phone Number:	
Date of First Meeting:	
Location:	
Topics to Discuss:	

Self Mail

Objectives   To reinforce and apply learning.

Materials
- One envelope per participant.

- Copy of *Self Mail* for each participant (p. 269).

Directions

1. Distribute an envelope to each participant.

2. Ask participants to address it to themselves.

3. Ask participants to record their improvement targets or some specific application that he/she intends to make—based on the program experience—on their participant handout, *Self Mail*.

4. Ask participants to put the *Self Mail* handout in the envelope and seal it.

5. Collect the sealed envelopes.

6. Tell participants when you will mail them—two or three weeks hence.

   Date to Mail: _____

Notes
- _____
- _____
- _____
- _____
- _____
- _____
- _____
- _____
- _____
- _____
- _____
- _____
- _____
- _____
- _____
- _____
- _____

HANDOUT	**Self Mail**
Objective	To reinforce and transfer learning to your job and work environment.
Directions	1. Complete this form.
	2. Seal it in the envelope that your trainer gives you.
	3. Address the envelope to yourself.
	4. Return it to your trainer.
	5. Look for it in the mail in two to three weeks.

I expect to use what I have learned in the program in the following ways:

I plan to learn more about the following:

I plan to describe to the following people what I learned in the program:

I plan to practice the following specific skills that I learned in the program:

Debriefing to Management

Objectives   To reinforce and apply learning.

Materials   • Copy of *Debriefing to Management* for each participant (p. 271).

Directions   Ask participants to write:

1. The name of a manager in their home organization.

2. A tentative date for the debriefing.

3. Specify what they learned from the program.

4. Specify what they intend to do with what they have learned.

Notes
• _____

• _____

• _____

• _____

• _____

• _____

• _____

• _____

• _____

• _____

• _____

• _____

• _____

• _____

• _____

• _____

• _____

• _____

• _____

• _____

• _____

HANDOUT	**Debriefing to Management**

Objectives To reinforce and transfer learning to your job and work environment.

Directions Fill in the following information:

Name of manager to be debriefed:

Date by which I intend to hold the debriefing:

Specific things I learned in the program:

Ways in which I might involve the manager in a mutual process to improve my coaching skills:

<u>**Trainer's Notes**</u>	# Workshop Evaluation—Short Form

Objectives

To evaluate the training program content and method, and your effectiveness as a trainer.

Materials

- Copy of *Workshop Evaluation —Short Form* for each participant (p. 273).

Directions

Distribute the form to participants of the one-hour training programs.

 One-hour training programs cannot carry the burden of a lengthy evaluation process, but you can gain valuable insights if you are evaluating a whole series of one-hour programs that you offered over a period of time.

Notes

- _____
- _____
- _____
- _____
- _____
- _____
- _____
- _____
- _____
- _____
- _____
- _____
- _____
- _____
- _____
- _____
- _____
- _____
- _____
- _____
- _____

HANDOUT	**Workshop Evaluation—Short Form**
Objectives	To evaluate the training program content and method, and the effectiveness of your trainer.
Directions	1. Complete this evaluation sheet before you leave the program.
	2. Return it to the person or location designated by your trainer.

Course Title: _____

Date: _____

Circle the number which represents your response to each item: **Disagree**   **Agree**

1. I received sufficient pre-workshop information
   to plan for and attend the program.   1   2   3   4   5

2. I was notified in sufficient time to plan properly
   for the program.   1   2   3   4   5

3. The training rooms were excellent.   1   2   3   4   5

4. The quality of training materials was excellent.   1   2   3   4   5

5. The quality of instruction was excellent.   1   2   3   4   5

6. My experience in the program has provided
   me with tools that can help me improve my performance.   1   2   3   4   5

7. I would recommend this program to others
   without reservation.   1   2   3   4   5

8. Comments:

   • _____

   • _____

   • _____

   • _____

   • _____

   • _____

   • _____

   • _____

   • _____

Workshop Evaluation—Long Form

Objectives

To evaluate the training program content and method, and your effectiveness as a trainer.

Materials

- Copy of *Workshop Evaluation—Long Form* for each participant (p. 275).

Directions

Distribute the form to participants of the half-, one-, two- and three-day training programs.

Notes

- _____

- _____

- _____

- _____

- _____

- _____

- _____

- _____

- _____

- _____

- _____

- _____

- _____

- _____

- _____

- _____

- _____

- _____

- _____

- _____

- _____

- _____

- _____

<u>H</u>ANDOUT	**Workshop Evaluation—Long Form**

Objectives	To evaluate the training program content and method, and the effectiveness of your trainer.

Directions	1. Complete this evaluation sheet before you leave the program.
	2. Return it to the person or location designated by your trainer.

Course Title: _____

Date: _____

Circle the number which represents your response to each item: Disagree   Agree

1. I received sufficient pre-workshop information to plan for and attend the program.   1   2   3   4   5

2. I was notified in sufficient time to plan properly for the program.   1   2   3   4   5

3. The training rooms were excellent.   1   2   3   4   5

4. Support during the program was excellent.   1   2   3   4   5

5. Make comments here, if you like, about administration of program and facilities:

- _____

- _____

- _____

- _____

- _____

Program

6. The quality of training materials was excellent.   1   2   3   4   5

7. The quality of instruction was excellent.   1   2   3   4   5

8. My experience in the program has provided me with tools that can help me improve my performance.   1   2   3   4   5

9. I would recommend this program to others without reservation.   1   2   3   4   5

10.   Make comments here, if you like, about the program:

- _____
- _____
- _____
- _____
- _____
- _____
- _____
- _____
- _____
- _____
- _____
- _____
- _____

Description of Overall Experience

11.   Write below short phrases or adjectives which describe your overall experience in this program:

- _____
- _____
- _____
- _____
- _____
- _____
- _____
- _____
- _____
- _____
- _____
- _____

Chapter Ten:

Using the Assessment Tools

This chapter contains assessment tools you can use to enrich your coaching training programs and validate their effectiveness.

> ## CHAPTER OVERVIEW
>
> This chapter contains the following assessment tools:
>
> - Coaching Behavior Analysis.
> - Coaching Values Questionnaire.
> - Coaching Skills Feedback Questionnaire.
> - The Follow-Up Interview and Questionnaire.
> - Pre- and Post- Videotaping.
>
> These tools can be used before, during, and after coaching training programs.

The assessment tools fall into two groups:

- **Personal Feedback Tools**

  Personal feedback tools give participants the means to establish their own levels of understanding and performance as coaches.

- **Organizational Impact Tools**

  Organizational impact tools give trainers the means to evaluate how coaching training has been transferred to personal and organizational performance.

Coaching Behavior Analysis (CBA)

Using the CBA

The *Coaching Behavior Analysis* provides the basis for a good discussion about good and poor coaching behaviors. You can relate the CBA to the Superior Coaching Model. To be a superior coach, coaching behavior must be congruent with the essential characteristics, the critical skills, and the core conversation.

Objectives

The purpose of the CBA is to permit individuals to assess their personal understanding of superior coaching behaviors. The CBA can be used as pre-work for a coaching program, as part of the training program or as a follow-up tool.

The key to this assessment tool is found after the CBA items.

Materials

• Copy of *Coaching Behavior Analysis* (p. 279).

HANDOUT   **Coaching Behavior Analysis (CBA)**

Directions   Assume you have a management or leadership responsibility for
                     the person described in the mini cases below. Circle the response
                     you think is most useful under the conditions described:

1.

> You have dropped in at the office of one of your employees
> as part of your "walking around" strategy. You ask the
> employee, "How are things going?" The employee says, "I
> don't think I am going to meet the planned schedule for the
> next design review."

You say:

   a. "That is going to throw the rest of our project off schedule."

   b. "You should have come to me about the problem as soon as
you thought you weren't going to make the schedule."

   c. "What sort of problems are you running into?"

   d. "How much of a delay do you expect?"

2.

> You have a colleague who is complaining to you about the
> lack of commitment in his team members.

Your response is:

   a. "Sounds like they have an attitude problem."

   b. "I think most people don't care as much as they used to
about doing a good job."

   c. "Do you think they would do a better job if they felt that it
was OK with you for them to make mistakes sometimes?"

   d. "What do you think it takes to build commitment?"

3.

> You have an employee who persistently makes grammatical mistakes in the reports that he/she writes. The employee is working on a report reviewing alternative plans for office automation. You have reviewed a draft and found several incomplete sentences, non-agreement in subjects and verbs, and mistakes in punctuation. You have called the employee in to discuss the problem.

During the conversation you would be most likely to say:

a. "It must be a case of carelessness. You seem to get things right most of the time, but then you have these lapses."

b. "Look at these two sentences. This one is a good, complete sentence. This other one is not. Using the first one as a model, see if you can fix the second one."

c. "When I reviewed this report, I had the sense that I was doing your job. I spend about as much time correcting your mistakes as it would take for me to write the report in the first place."

d. "Here is the report with the mistakes marked in red. Please go back and correct them and bring it back to me this afternoon."

Answer key

1. Responses "c" and "d" suggest a strong commitment to coaching. Both try to explore the problem, rather than attack the employee. Both responses help create the essential condition of respect and both examples use the critical skill of inquiring.

2. Responses "c" and "d" suggest a clear understanding of the conditions that build commitment. Responses "a" and "b" suggest a weak understanding.

3. Response "b" suggests that the respondent sees the situation as an opportunity for teaching and has a strong commitment to coaching. The other responses suggest that the respondent does not see the situation as an opportunity for teaching.

<u>HANDOUT</u>

Coaching Values Questionnaire (CVQ)

Using the CVQ

The CVQ measures an individual's self-perception about the way they value coaching. The CVQ is best used in connection with discussions about key values in a training program. Participants can fill out the CVQ before they attend a program, or at the beginning of a program. You can also modify the CVQ and use it to obtain feedback from coworkers.

Directions

To what degree do you believe that the following statements are characteristic of your behaviors or performance? Circle the number that you believe applies to you for each statement.

Answer key

1 = very characteristic, 2 = moderately characteristic,
3 = somewhat characteristic, 4 = moderately uncharacteristic,
5 = very uncharacteristic

	High			**Low**

In relationships with employees and coworkers:

	High			Low
1. I show them I believe that they desire to be fully competent in their jobs.	1	2	3	4	5
2. I give them the chance to demonstrate their competence.	1	2	3	4	5
3. I encourage them to take on increasingly challenging tasks.	1	2	3	4	5
4. I make minimum use of controls.	1	2	3	4	5
5. I am quick to express appreciation for their good work.	1	2	3	4	5
6. I give them every opportunity to improve when they make a mistake.	1	2	3	4	5
7. I make sure their work is as challenging as I can make it.	1	2	3	4	5
8. I am easily available to talk with about improving performance.	1	2	3	4	5
9. I make it easy for them to tell me if they don't know how to do something.	1	2	3	4	5
10. I often initiate conversations to help them perform at their top potential.	1	2	3	4	5

<u>HANDOUT</u>

Coaching Skills Feedback Questionnaire (CSFQ)

Using the CSFQ

The CSFQ is a dual purpose feedback instrument that participants use to:

- Obtain feedback from their coworkers prior to a coaching training program.

- Assess their performance as coaches after attending a coaching training program.

To obtain useful information, at least five coworkers should give feedback and only 4's and 5's represent a clearly positive rating. The numbers are far less important than the feedback, which leads to thinking of ways to improve one's coaching performance.

Directions

The name of the person I am evaluating is: _____

To what degree do you believe that the following statements are characteristic of the person about whom you are completing this questionnaire? Circle the number that you believe applies to that person for each statement.

Answer key

1 = very characteristic, 2 = moderately characteristic,
3 = somewhat characteristic, 4 = moderately uncharacteristic,
5 = very uncharacteristic

	High			Low

In relationships with employees and coworkers:

1. Shows coworkers that he/she believes they want to be fully competent in their jobs.	1	2	3	4	5
2. Gives coworkers the chance to demonstrate their competence.	1	2	3	4	5
3. Encourages coworkers to take on more challenging tasks.	1	2	3	4	5
4. Makes minimum use of controls to manage coworkers' performance.	1	2	3	4	5
5. Is quick to express appreciation for coworkers' good work.	1	2	3	4	5
6. Gives coworkers every opportunity to improve when they make mistakes.	1	2	3	4	5
7. Makes sure work of coworkers is as challenging as he/she can make it.	1	2	3	4	5

Coaching Skills Feedback Questionnaire (continued)

8. Is easily available to talk to about improving performance.   1   2   3   4   5

9. Makes it easy for coworkers to tell him/her they don't know how to do something.   1   2   3   4   5

10. Often initiates conversations to help coworkers perform at their top potential.   1   2   3   4   5

Notes

- _____
- _____
- _____
- _____
- _____
- _____
- _____
- _____
- _____
- _____
- _____
- _____
- _____
- _____
- _____
- _____
- _____

<u>HANDOUT</u>   # The Follow-Up Interview

Overview

Interviews may be conducted in person or by telephone between two and four weeks after the program. The three questions below can help you make a judgment about what participants learned from the program and if they have applied what they learned.

Administrative

(To be completed before the interview)

Name: _____

Phone: _____

Date of program attended: _____

Length of program: _____

Program content

1. What information, ideas, skills or other content do you remember that were covered or discussed in the program you attended on coaching?

    If the interviewee does not offer specific information about the Superior Coaching Model, go to question 2.

2. Can you describe the Superior Coaching Model that was covered in the program? (The interviewee might want to draw the model.)

Application of learning

3. Can you recall any specific times that you have consciously tried to apply any of the ideas or skills that were covered in the program? (Help the interviewee become as specific as possible.)

The Follow-Up Questionnaire

Overview

This questionnaire should be conducted between one and two weeks after the program. It determines how much of the program's content the participants remember (they must have learned it to remember it). Indicate in your cover letter that the questionnaire is anonymous and that participants should answer the questionnaire without reference to any notes.

Directions

1. What are the elements included in the Superior Coaching Model?

2. What are the essential characteristics of a coaching conversation that are included in the Superior Coaching Model and which are characteristic of superior coaching conversations?

3. What are the critical skills included in the Superior Coaching Model that superior coaches characteristically use?

TRAINER'S NOTES

Pre- and Post- Program Videotaping

Overview

In this assessment, a number of persons attending the program are matched with the same number of persons who did not attend the program. It is not necessary to use all the participants. If you use a random sample of 25% percent in a program of 18 to 20 people, you can obtain a good indication of the results of the program.

Directions

1. Select any of the extended interaction exercises from Chapter 9.

2. During the taping, allow those who attended the program—as well as those who did not—serve as the coach.

3. Use the observation sheets after the taped interview is completed.

4. Use at least three qualified observers to record the performance of the subjects on the observation sheets.

5. By summarizing and averaging the information on the observation sheets, you can develop an evaluation of the performance of those attending and those not attending the program.

6. The results from the two groups can be compared to demonstrate the degree of learning that took place in the program.

Chapter Eleven:

Overhead Transparencies

This chapter contains overhead transparencies for all coaching workshops—ready to go "as is" or to be tailored to meet your needs.

USING THE OVERHEAD TRANSPARENCIES

You may use the overhead transparencies in four ways:

- Key them into your word processing system "as is" or customize them to suit your specific needs.

- Photocopy the overhead transparency masters that you need from this book and use them "as is."

- Photocopy the masters on plain paper and distribute them as handouts.

- Create flipcharts by handlettering the content on sheets of 2' x 3' chart paper.

Although these visual aids are called overheads, they can obviously be made into charts—either before a program or by trainers as they lead an interactive presentation or conduct a review/preview.

You will find it useful to make copies of your overheads and include them in the materials for participants. If you produce a participant's notebook, you will logically place overheads in the notebook in the order in which they are referred to in the program.

Overheads

The chapter includes the following overheads:

Introductory
- (Workshop Title and Trainer's Name)
- *Changes in Management and Leadership Functions*

Objectives
- *Objectives for One-Hour Program: The Superior Coaching Model*
- *Objectives for One-Hour Program: The Critical Skills of Superior Coaching*
- *Objectives for Half-Day Program: Introduction To Superior Coaching*
- *Objectives for One-Day Workshop*
- *Objectives for Two-Day Workshop*
- *Objectives for Three-Day Workshop*

Program flow
- *Half-Day Program Flow*
- *One-Day Program Flow*
- *Two-Day Program Flow*
- *Three-Day Program Flow*
- *Program Norms*
- *Why Coaching Is Becoming So Important*
- *The Meaning of Superior Coaching*
- *The Superior Coaching Model*
- *The Core Conversation*
- *The Four Performance Applications*
- *What Superior Coaches Believe*
- *Essential Characteristics*
- *The Meaning of Balance*
- *The Meaning of Being Concrete*
- *The Meaning of Respect*
- *Critical Skills*

Performance applications
- *Resolving Problems Performance Application*
- *Teaching Performance Application*
- *Supporting Performance Application*
- *Adjusting Performance Application*
- *Review and Action Teams*

SUPERIOR COACHING TRAINING PROGRAM

Welcome!

Your trainer is:

Changes in Management and Leadership Functions

From leading and managing through:

- Direct oversight.
- Directing.
- Limiting performance.
- Individuals.

To leading and managing through:

- Indirect oversight.
- Setting values/goals.
- Empowering.
- Teams.

OBJECTIVES FOR ONE-HOUR PROGRAM

The Superior Coaching Model:

- Familiarize participants with the Superior Coaching Model.

- Ensure participants understand each of the elements in the model.

- Ensure participants understand how the elements of the model are related to each other.

OBJECTIVES FOR ONE-HOUR PROGRAM

The Critical Skills of Superior Coaching:

- Reinforce participants' understanding of the Superior Coaching Model.

- Familiarize participants with the five critical skills of superior coaching.

OBJECTIVES FOR HALF-DAY PROGRAM

Introduction to Superior Coaching:

- Understand the importance of coaching as a leadership role.

- Introduce the Superior Coaching Model.

- Minimum understanding and skills to use the Superior Coaching Model.

OBJECTIVES FOR ONE-DAY WORKSHOP

The Superior Coaching Model:

- Understand the importance of coaching as a leadership role.

- Introduce the Superior Coaching Model.

- Minimum understanding and skills to use the Superior Coaching Model.

Objectives for Two-Day Workshop

- Understand the importance of coaching as a leadership role.

- Understand the Superior Coaching Model.

- Equip you with the minimum skills to use the Superior Coaching Model.

- Feedback on how well you apply the Superior Coaching Model.

- Plan to reinforce your learning after the program and apply what you have learned to your job.

Objectives for Three-Day Workshop

- Understand the importance of coaching as a leadership role.

- Understand the Superior Coaching Model.

- Understand each element in the model and how all the elements are related to each other.

- Equip you with all the skills required to use the Superior Coaching Model.

- Feedback on how well you apply the Superior Coaching Model.

- Plan to reinforce your learning after the program and apply what you have learned to your job.

HALF-DAY PROGRAM FLOW

- The importance of coaching.

- The meaning of superior coaching.

- Superior Coaching Model.

- Critical skills for superior coaching.

ONE-DAY PROGRAM FLOW

- The importance of coaching.

- Introduce the Superior Coaching Model.

- Clarify meaning of all elements in model.

- Skill practice.

Two-Day Program Flow

Day One:

- The importance of coaching.

- Organize review and action teams.

- Introduce the Superior Coaching Model.

- Clarify meaning of all elements in model.

- Action planning to reinforce and apply learning.

TWO-DAY PROGRAM FLOW
(CONTINUED)

Day Two:

- Continue to clarify meaning of all elements in model.

- Skill practice.

- Continue action planning to reinforce and apply learning.

- Practice skills in two extended interactions.

THREE-DAY PROGRAM FLOW

Day One:

- The importance of coaching.

- Organize review and action teams.

- Introduce the Superior Coaching Model.

- Clarify meaning of all elements in model.

- Begin action planning to reinforce and apply learning.

THREE-DAY PROGRAM FLOW

(CONTINUED)

Day Two:

- Continue to clarify meaning of all elements in model.

- Begin skill practice.

- Continue action planning to reinforce and apply learning.

Day Three:

- Continue skill practice.

- Practice skills in two extended interactions.

PROGRAM NORMS

- Informal and interactive.

- Take each other's comments and questions seriously.

- Listen to understand.

- Avoid nitpicking.

- No sub-grouping.

- Be prompt.

- Have fun.

WHY COACHING IS BECOMING SO IMPORTANT

- Control model for managing and leading isn't working all that well.

- Present need is to do more with less and empower people.

- Managers and leaders are being expected to act as resources and problem solvers.

- Coaching is a primary tool for being a resource and solving problems.

The Meaning of Superior Coaching

- Successful coaching is an activity that results in the continuous improvement of performance.

- Coaching is a conversation between a leader and an individual or a team that results in the continuous improvement of performance.

- Coaching is a disciplined conversation, using concrete performance information, that takes place between a leader and an individual or a team that results in the continuous improvement of performance.

THE SUPERIOR COACHING MODEL

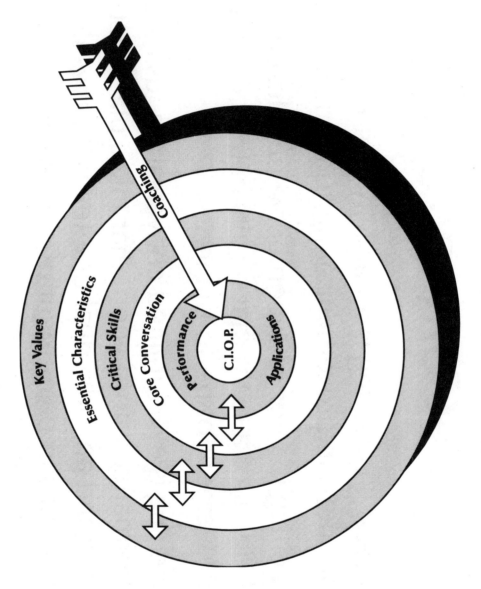

Key Values

Essential Characteristics

Critical Skills

Core Conversation

Coaching

Performance

C.I.O.P.

Applications

C.I.O.P. = Continuous Improvement of Performance

The Core Conversation

THE FOUR PERFORMANCE APPLICATIONS

- Resolving Problems.

- Teaching.

- Supporting Performance.

- Adjusting Performance.

WHAT SUPERIOR COACHES BELIEVE

About Human Competency:

- People want to be competent, and given help, will strive to be more competent.

- People must be given the opportunity to demonstrate competency in order to gain competency.

About Superior Performance:

- Managing and leading by control is not practical and does not lead to superior performance.

- Superior performance results from the commitment of individuals and teams to be superior.

WHAT SUPERIOR COACHES BELIEVE

(CONTINUED)

Commitment Results When People:

- Are clear about what they are doing and what is important.

- Have the competencies to perform the jobs that are expected of them.

- Feel appreciated for what they do.

- Feel challenged by their jobs.

- Have the chance to improve when they make mistakes.

About the Value of Coaching:

- Must initiate coaching interactions.

- Must be disciplined.

310

ESSENTIAL CHARACTERISTICS

- Balance.

- Being concrete.

- Shared responsibility.

- Shape.

- Respect.

THE MEANING OF BALANCE

Superior coaching is not one sided.
There is give and take, questioning, and sharing
of information and ideas. All parties are fully involved.

Balance is what a superior coach creates through
skilled and disciplined behavior.

THE MEANING OF BEING CONCRETE

Focuses on

the objective and descriptive

aspects of performance.

THE MEANING OF RESPECT

Demonstrating respect is no more complicated than avoiding behaviors which communicate that a person is stupid, or evil, or inferior, or some such; and using behaviors in a conversation which involve the other person and make that person a fully accepted player.

CRITICAL SKILLS

- Attending.
- Inquiring.
- Reflecting.
- Affirming.
- Being Disciplined.

RESOLVING PROBLEMS
PERFORMANCE APPLICATION

Expanding Phase:

- Mutual understanding of problem or problems.

- Mutual understanding of the history of the problem.

- Mutual understanding of the causes of the problem.

- Mutual understanding of the implications, if problem is not resolved.

RESOLVING PROBLEMS
PERFORMANCE APPLICATION

(CONTINUED)

Focusing Phase:

- Mutually develop alternative strategies for resolving the problem.

- Mutually agree on plan to resolve the problem.

- Mutually agree on follow-up plan to track progress.

TEACHING

PERFORMANCE APPLICATION

Expanding Phase:

- Mutual understanding of what the coach wants the other person to learn, i.e., the goals of the conversation.

- Mutual understanding of what the other person already knows.

- Mutual understanding of how the conversation will proceed, i.e., what is the sequence, what will happen first, second, and so forth.

TEACHING

PERFORMANCE APPLICATION

(CONTINUED)

Focusing Phase:

- Teach the content that the other person needs to learn.

- Check to ensure (by feedback or demonstration) that learning has occurred.

- Clear up any residual questions that the other person has.

SUPPORTING
PERFORMANCE APPLICATION

Expanding Phase:

- Clear description of performance being discussed.

- Clarification of expectations concerning the performance.

- Mutual understanding of importance of the performance.

SUPPORTING
PERFORMANCE APPLICATION
(CONTINUED)

Focusing Phase:

- Giving feedback about the performance.

- Mutual agreement about changes in performance requirements or expectations.

- Expressing appreciation for performance.

321

ADJUSTING
PERFORMANCE APPLICATION

Expanding Phase:

- Specific performance being discussed.

- Concrete statement of what the coach believes to be the problem in performance.

- The other person's understanding of the problem.

- Agreement concerning the nature of the performance problem.

- Clarity about who is responsible for resolving the problem.

- Alternative strategies for resolving the problem.

ADJUSTING
PERFORMANCE APPLICATION
(CONTINUED)

Focusing Phase:

- Agreement on what performance will be adjusted and to what degree.

- Agreement on plan to adjust performance.

- Agreement on a follow-up plan to monitor progress.

Review and Action Teams

- Meet as indicated by facilitator during program.

- Share and reinforce their learning.

- Raise questions that they need answered.

- If possible, continue to meet after program.

Recommended Resources

Blanchard, Kenneth H. 1992. "How to Turn Around Department Performance." *Supervisory Management* (March): 3-5.

A useful description of the positive results that can be achieved by developing coaching skills in supervisors.

Crane, Janet G. 1991. "Getting the Performance You Want." *Association Management* (February): 24-30.

Demonstrates how coaching is a more effective means of managing performance than traditional controlling and directing behaviors.

Frankel, Lois P.; Otazo, Karen L. 1992. "Employee Coaching: the Way to Gain Commitment, Not Just Compliance." *Employment Relations Today* (Autumn): 311-320.

Shows how coaching develops clarity about performance goals and commitment to these goals.

Geber, Beverly. 1992. "From Manager into Coach." *Training* (February): 25-31.

An overview of the general movement away from managing by directing and controlling to managing by becoming a resource and problem-solver.

Halson, Bill. 1990. "Teaching Supervisors to Coach." *Personnel Management* (March): 36-39.

Provides some useful ideas about how to train supervisors to be coaches and gives practical suggestions for the kinds of activities that help train coaches.

Kinlaw, Dennis C. 1990. *Coaching for Commitment: Trainer's Package*. San Diego: University Associates.

A complete training program in coaching. Provides video behavior models to demonstrate the major coaching functions.

Kinlaw, Dennis C. 1991. *Developing Superior Work Teams: Building Quality and the Competitive Edge*. Lexington, Mass.: Lexington Books.

Describes an empirical basis for superior teams. Identifies coaching as a major function performed by leaders of superior teams.

Kinlaw, Dennis C. 1990. *Coaching Skills Inventory*. San Diego: University Associates.

A feedback instrument that correlates coaching behavior with the performance of superior managers and leaders. Has a self report form and a form for gathering feedback from others.

Kinlaw, Dennis C. 1989. *Coaching for Commitment; Managerial Strategies for Obtaining Superior Performance*. San Diego: University Associates.

Gives a specific meaning to the concept of coaching and provides a detailed description of the interactive and interpersonal dimensions of coaching.

McKenna, Joseph F. 1992. "Coach Lets His Team Play the Game (Employee Empowerment Works Wonders for Picker International, Manufacturer of High-tech X-ray Equipment)." *Industry Week* (May 4): 12-14.

Gives a proven application of coaching as a major strategy to empower people and improve the bottom line.

Ottele, Richard G.; Schaefer, Barbara A. 1991. "How to Provide Effective On the Job Coaching for Your Staff." *The Practical Accountant* (January): 70-73.

Gives practical guidance for using coaching as a way to improve performance, and identifies the opportunities for coaching on the job.

Quick, Thomas L. 1990. "Curbstone Coaching." *Sales and Marketing Management* (July): 100-101.

Shows how coaching can be used to give immediate help in training salespersons. Emphasizes the teaching and mentoring functions of coaching.

Sturman, Gerald M. 1990. "The Supervisor as Career Coach." *Supervisory Management* (November): 6-8.

Relates coaching directly to the process of developing people. Shows how coaching should be an integral part of any career development program.

Index

About the Author

Dennis C. Kinlaw, Ed. D., has served as organization and management education consultant to over fifty public and private organizations. Clients have included: The Aerospace Corporation, The Bell Atlantic Corporation, Lawrence Livermore National Laboratory, NASA Headquarters, NASA Kennedy Space Center, MCI, General Electric, EG&G, Quad/Graphics, United States Coast Guard, Zenger/Miller, The National Institute of Health, and the Health Care Finance Administration.

He has served as faculty or adjunct faculty for Virginia Commonwealth University, The American University, The George Washington University, and McCormick Theological Seminary.

Dr. Kinlaw is the only private management consultant to have received the Public Service Medal from NASA for consulting and training services.

In addition to some fifty articles, Dr. Kinlaw is the author of the following books:

Listening and Responding, Pfeiffer & Company, 1981

Coaching for Commitment, Pfeiffer & Company, 1989

Trainer's Package, Coaching for Commitment, Pfeiffer & Company, 1990

Developing Superior Work Teams, Lexington Books, 1991

Continuous Improvement and Measurement for Total Quality, Business One Irwin, 1992

Team Managed Facilitation, Pfeiffer and Company, 1993

Measurement Planning Handbook, NASA, 1993

Measurement Planning Workbook, NASA, 1993

The Practice of Empowerment, Gower, 1995

Trainer's Package: Superior Team Development Workshop, HRD Press, 1995